How To...

BY STEVE GORENBURG

CREATE ROCK BASS LINES

PLAYBACK+
Speed • Pitch • Balance • Loop

To access audio visit:
www.halleonard.com/mylibrary

Enter Code
7951-1591-0094-4237

ISBN 978-1-4950-4741-1

HAL•LEONARD®
CORPORATION
7777 W. BLUEMOUND RD. P.O. BOX 13819 MILWAUKEE, WI 53213

In Australia Contact:
Hal Leonard Australia Pty. Ltd.
4 Lentara Court
Cheltenham, Victoria, 3192 Australia
Email: ausadmin@halleonard.com.au

Visit Hal Leonard Online at
www.halleonard.com

CONTENTS

INTRODUCTION

The function of the bass player in rock music is multi-dimensional. A successful bass line can act as the glue that binds the rhythm, harmony, and melody together, while complementing all three elements. The bass is an integral part of the rhythm section, and learning how to play a solid groove is essential. An effective bass player will be familiar with the notes on the neck, chords, and scales, enabling him to complement the vocals, guitar, and keyboards, all while staying married to the drum beat.

In this book, you'll explore common rock drum beats and how to lock in with them, popular rock chord progressions, and the scales and techniques you'll need to add melody to your playing. By combining all of these elements, you'll learn how to create your own bass lines that will stand out while still locking in with the drums and complementing the other instruments and vocals. We'll also take a look at the styles of some of the rock bass greats like Paul McCartney, John Paul Jones, Flea, John Entwistle, and Duff McKagan.

AUDIO

Music examples accompany the lessons, so you can hear what each example sounds like. Backing tracks are also provided so you can jam along. To access all of the audio examples that accompany this book, simply go to **www.halleonard.com/mylibrary** and enter the code found on page 1. The examples that include audio are marked with an icon throughout the book.

Special thanks to guitarist Chris Declercq for supplying the guitar parts featured on the audio tracks.

ABOUT THE AUTHOR

Steve Gorenberg is a bass player, music educator, author, arranger, transcriber, and music engraver based in Los Angeles. Steve started out at Cherry Lane Music's print division as a transcriber and in-house music editor. He has since continued as a freelance transcriber, editor, and engraver for Cherry Lane Music, *Guitar for the Practicing Musician* magazine, Hal Leonard Corp., Fred Russell Publishing, and Warner Bros. Inc., and has written, edited, and designed numerous music education products. To date, Steve has created thousands of official note-for-note guitar and bass transcriptions for artists including Metallica, Guns N' Roses, the Red Hot Chili Peppers, the Rolling Stones, Van Halen, Pearl Jam, Rush, Black Sabbath, Queen, and John Mayer.

HOW TO USE THIS BOOK

For each lesson chapter, listen to the audio track and try playing along with the music examples. When you've got them down, use the scales and ideas presented to create your own bass lines. The last section contains play-along tracks that showcase many of the drum beats and chord progressions used throughout the book. You can create your own bass lines for these tracks using all of the elements presented in the previous chapters.

FINDING THE BEAT

At its very core, the bass is an essential part of the rhythm section. Any effective bass line is sure to lock in with the drummer, so the beat is a good place to start. Some of the simplest bass parts work extremely well when they follow the kick drum. The song "Dreams" by Fleetwood Mac comes to mind—the bass plays simple root notes along with the kick-drum pattern but still manages to create one of the most recognizable rock bass lines of all time. In this chapter, we'll concentrate on following the beat using mostly root notes to get you accustomed to commonly used rock drum patterns. Once you've developed an instinct for listening to the drummer and following the beat, you'll be able to add melody and riffs to your playing while keeping the groove intact.

Basic Rock Beats

Let's begin with a basic rock drum beat, shown below in music notation. For the purposes of this book, we'll indicate drums on a musical staff using x's for noteheads. The downstemmed notes represent the kick drum, and the upstemmed notes represent the snare drum. The kick and snare pattern is the most important thing to listen for when building your bass lines, so don't be concerned with what the cymbals or other drums are doing at this point.

Rock Beat #1

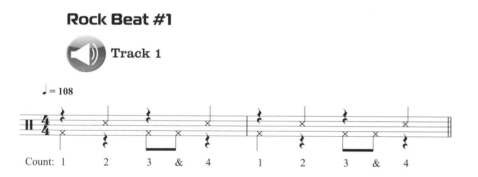

The following example is a simple two-chord progression, with the bass playing just the root notes, A and G, along with the above beat. Concentrate on memorizing and locking in with the kick drum pattern.

Now let's create a slight variation of the previous drum beat by adding an extra kick drum to beat 4 1/2.

Rock Beat #2

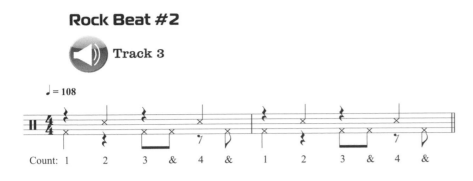

Track 3

Here's a variation of the previous bass line, adding a note on beat 4 1/2 of each measure.

Track 4

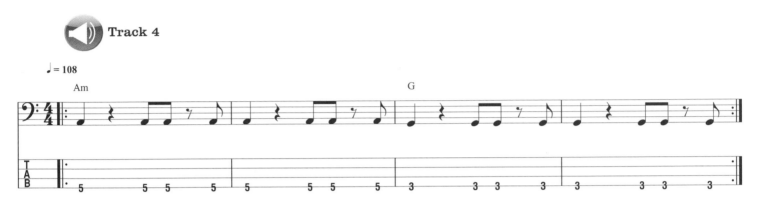

This next example uses the same beat and adds bass notes for the snare-drum hits. In most rock music, the snare drum is played on beats 2 and 4—i.e., the same beats you would clap on. These notes are shown below using accents in the notation for reading convenience. You don't need to heavily accent these notes when you play them, but adding a little extra kick to them will help you lock in better with the groove.

Track 5

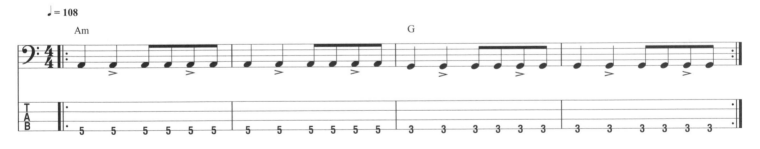

This next example is played to the same beat and adds a few other note choices to create a slightly more interesting bass line.

Track 6

The following example has a solid kick drum on beats 1 and 3, but also places a kick drum on beat 2 1/2. This drum pattern and the variations that follow are commonly used, steady rock beats.

Rock Beat #3

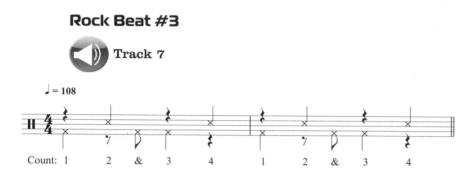
Track 7

Here's a simple bass line that follows the above kick drum pattern.

Track 8

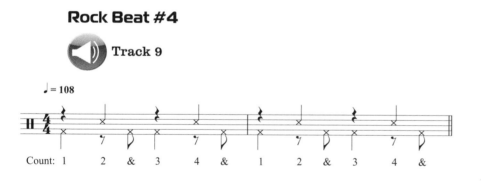

Let's take the previous beat and place an additional kick drum on beat 4 1/2.

Rock Beat #4

Track 9

Here's an accompanying bass line that incorporates open-string transitional notes, plus a few additional notes to accent some of the snare hits.

Track 10

This next beat adds another kick drum to beat 3 1/2 of the previous pattern.

Rock Beat #5

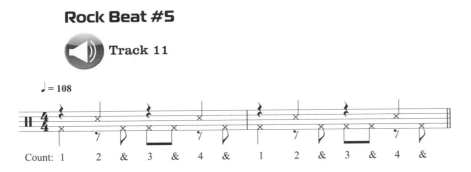

Track 11

♩ = 108

Count: 1   2 & 3 & 4 &   1   2 & 3 & 4 &

The following bass line locks in with the kick drum in the above beat. The chords change twice per measure in this progression.

Track 12

♩ = 108

Now let's start making these beats a little more interesting. This next example places a kick drum one 16th note before beat 3, functioning as a pick-up into the downbeat.

Rock Beat #6

Track 13

♩ = 102

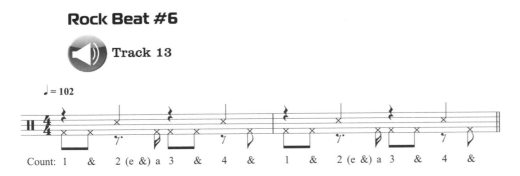

Count: 1 & 2 (e &) a 3 & 4 &   1 & 2 (e &) a 3 & 4 &

This bass line follows the above kick and snare pattern, playing mostly root notes on the kick drums and octaves on the snare hits.

Track 14

♩ = 102

This next beat is a variation of the previous one with a kick drum placed on beat 4 1/4.

Rock Beat #7

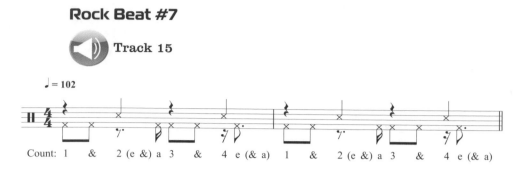

Track 15

Here's a bass line that follows most of the downbeats with root notes and uses some different note choices to accent the additional off-beat kick drums.

Track 16

Syncopation

A *syncopated* rhythm is one that stresses the off-beats, instead of the typical downbeats (beats 1, 2, 3, and 4). Syncopation occurs when we place the emphasis on the upbeats instead of the downbeats.

In the following example, the traditional downbeat at the beginning of the second measure has been moved back to the "and" of beat 4 of the first measure. This is one of the most basic forms of syncopation that you'll often encounter.

Rock Beat #8

Track 17

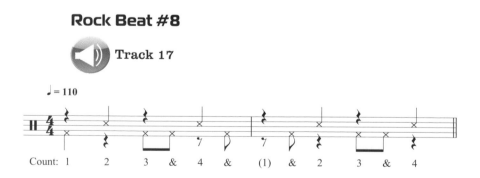

The following progression and bass line demonstrates this form of syncopation by changing chords on the "and" of beat 4 in every other measure. Besides the use of syncopation, this is an otherwise straight-forward, eighth-note bass line.

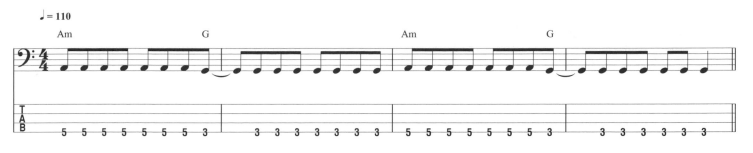

We can expand on the previous example of syncopation by moving the downbeat on beat 3 back to the "and" of beat 2 in each measure, as shown in the following drum pattern.

Rock Beat #9

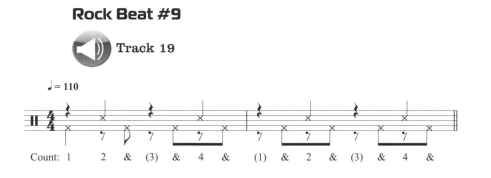

This next bass line follows the above pattern by changing chords on the syncopated beats.

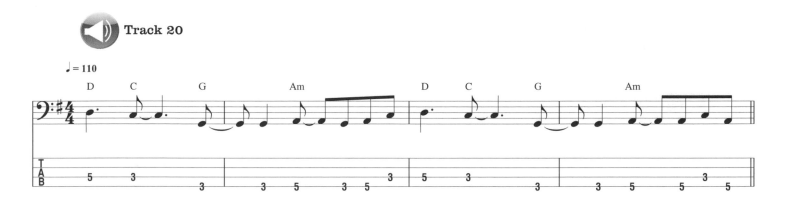

Keep in mind that it's often preferable to leave space between the notes by using rests. A "choked" note in time with the kick drum can have a more solid effect. Here's an example that combines elements of the previous two beats.

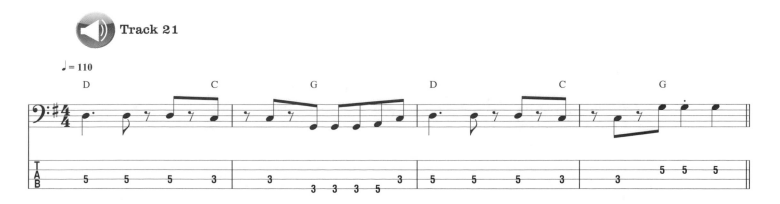

In this next example, the syncopation starts on the "and" of beat 1 and continues through all of the upbeats until resolving on beat 3 of the second measure.

Rock Beat #10

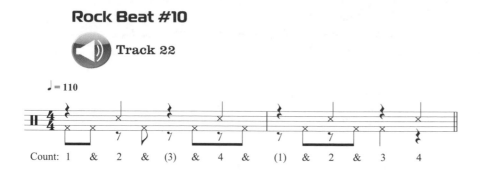

This next bass line follows the above kick drum pattern and is similar to the groove heard in Ted Nugent's "Stranglehold."

Track 23

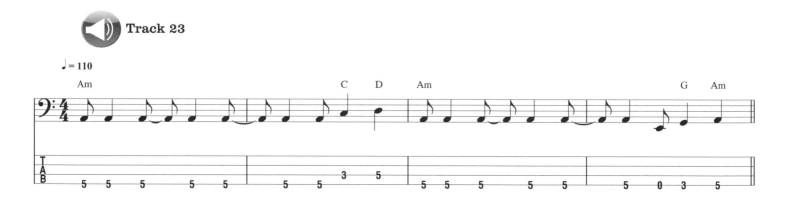

Here's a variation of the same bass line that adds octaves to the snare drum hits on beats 2 and 4.

Track 24

Some of the bass lines presented so far may seem simplistic in their strict adherence to the drum patterns. Keep in mind that these examples have been designed to help you develop an awareness of the beat and an instinct for following the drummer. Playing root notes on every kick drum or octaves on every snare drum may help to establish a solid rhythm section, but it may not sound very interesting. Rhythm is only one element of a successful, creative bass line, and in subsequent chapters, you'll learn how to add melody and riffs while keeping the groove intact.

The next few beats are examples of a funkier style of syncopation reminiscent of songs by Aerosmith and Guns N' Roses. The first beat starts out with a dotted eighth note followed by a tied 16th note.

Rock Beat #11

Track 25

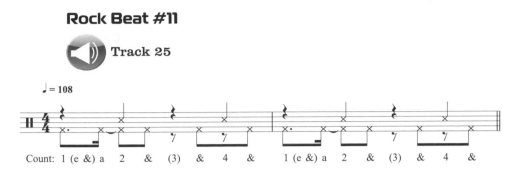

Count: 1 (e &) a 2 & (3) & 4 &   1 (e &) a 2 & (3) & 4 &

Here's a bass line to go with that beat. This example has a similar sound to Guns N' Roses' "Mr. Brownstone."

Track 26

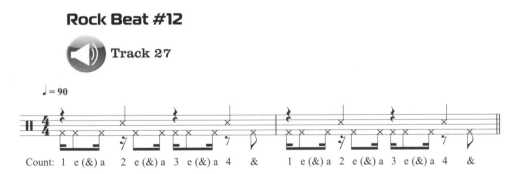

This next rhythm features a 16th-eighth-16th note phrase for the first three beats. The eighth note in the middle of each beat is slightly accented to create the syncopation.

Rock Beat #12

Track 27

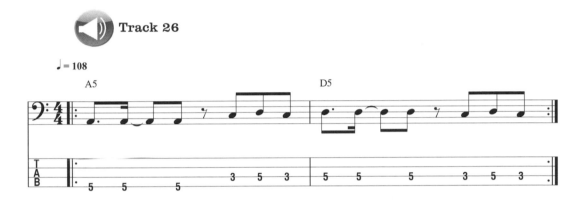

Count: 1 e (&) a 2 e (&) a 3 e (&) a 4 &   1 e (&) a 2 e (&) a 3 e (&) a 4 &

This bass line follows the above beat and is similar to one of the riffs from Aerosmith's "Sweet Emotion."

Track 28

Four-on-the-floor

The term *four-on-the-floor* refers to a steady, uniform rhythm in which the kick drum is played on every downbeat. The snare drum can be present on beats 2 & 4, or it can be omitted entirely for the sake of dynamics. Four-on-the-floor was made popular in disco and electronic dance music, but you'll also encounter it in rock and reggae songs. Here's a basic four-on-the-floor beat.

Rock Beat #13

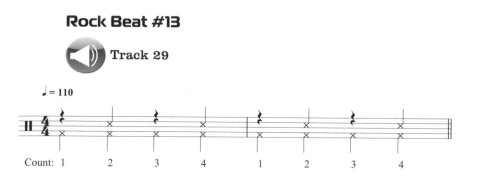

Here's a simple rock bass line to go with the above beat. Besides the basic downbeats, we've added a few eighth notes in between to make it a little more interesting.

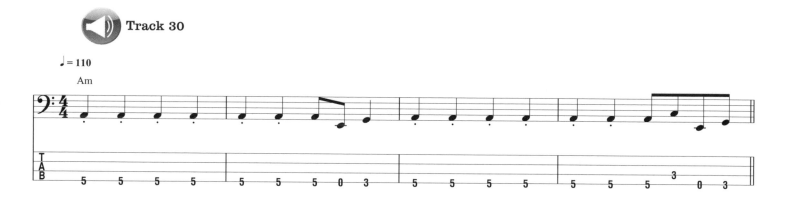

An obvious bass choice for four-on-the-floor is to play octaves on the upbeats. When combined with a walking bass melody, it definitely sounds disco. However, disco influences have been used in many rock and metal songs since the '70s. "Miss You," by the Rolling Stones, and "I Was Made for Loving You" by Kiss are both good examples. Even Ozzy's "Crazy Train" uses a four-on-the-floor beat during the verses.

One of the great things about four-on-the-floor is that the drummer is single-handedly holding down the pulse, with the kick drum acting like a metronome. This gives the bass plenty of room to create a groove using riffs and melodies. The following example features a busier, funkier bass line played against the same four-on-the-floor beat.

 **Track 32**

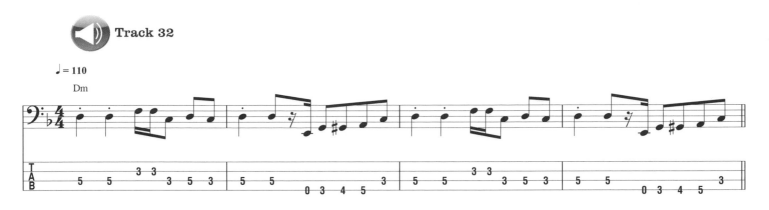

6/8 and 12/8 Time

The use of 6/8 time has become increasingly popular in all styles of rock music. This meter contains six eighth notes per measure, with the emphasis on the first and fourth eighth notes, essentially dividing the measure in half (two groups of three eighth notes per measure). In 6/8 time, you are more or less counting in triplet groups: "*one*-two-three, *four*-five-six." Here's a simple 6/8 rock beat. Notice that the snare drum hits are on the fourth eighth note of each measure (the perceived second downbeat in each measure).

Rock Beat #14

 **Track 33**

This next bass line goes along with the above 6/8 beat. Here, the bass plays simple root notes in time with the drum beat. Once you've got the groove down, you can easily add more melody to this line.

 **Track 34**

Similar to 6/8 time, 12/8 time is counted in triplet groups (four groups of three eighth notes). Many slow blues songs are played in 12/8 time. The examples below show 12/8 time initially counted as 12 eighth notes, with the perceived downbeats in bold type, and then as four groups of triplets (*One*-and-a, *two*-and-a, etc.), as you should probably count it.

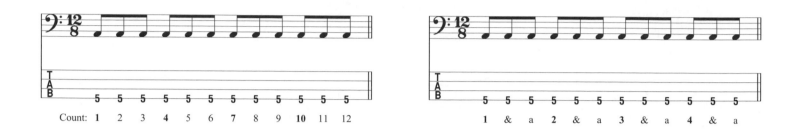

Here's a typical 12/8 drum beat. Notice the similarity to the previous 6/8 beat.

Rock Beat #15

Track 35

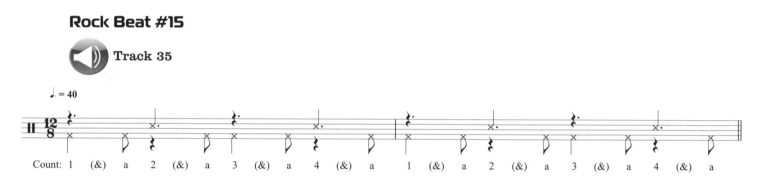

Here's a slow blues bass line in the key of A minor, written in 12/8 time. Some examples of slow blues songs in 12/8 are "Since I've Been Loving You" by Led Zeppelin and "Red House" by Jimi Hendrix.

Track 36

Shuffle Feel

Many rock and blues songs are played with a *shuffle feel*. In a shuffle feel, the second eighth note of each beat lags a little. Technically, it's the same as dividing each beat into a triplet, but only playing the first and third notes of the triplet, as shown below.

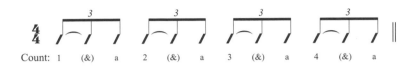

Count: 1 (&) a   2 (&) a   3 (&) a   4 (&) a

Instead of showing shuffle feel using triplets, it's usually written out as regular eighth notes, but with the following equivalency indicated at the beginning of the song, telling you that the eighths should be played in a shuffle feel.

You'll encounter the shuffle feel in all styles of rock music—from blues to rockabilly to metal. Even bands like Black Sabbath have used shuffle feels extensively. Here's a basic drum beat played in a shuffle feel. Notice that you can still count "one-and, two-and," etc., but do so with a shuffle feel.

Rock Beat #16

🔊 **Track 37**

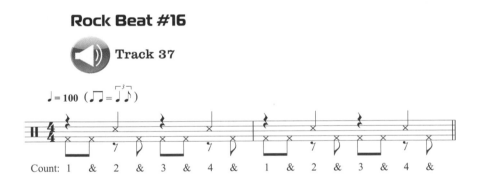

Count: 1 & 2 & 3 & 4 &   1 & 2 & 3 & 4 &

Here's a simple eighth-note bass line played with a shuffle feel. Since the shuffle rhythm is based on a triplet feel, you can use triplets to play fills. This line is similar to "Roadhouse Blues" by The Doors.

🔊 **Track 38**

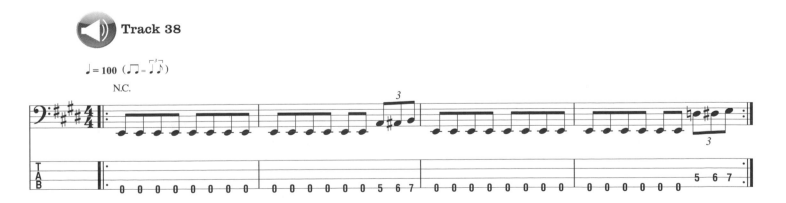

Shuffle feel can be found in a lot of old-school rock and R&B music. Here's a typical example using a version of the standard I–IV–V chord progression. We'll explore more variations of this chord change in future chapters.

Track 39

Sometimes a shuffle drum beat will only have kick and snare hits on the quarter-note downbeats, especially at very fast tempos. In cases like this, you'll need to listen to what the hi-hat or ride cymbals are doing to determine if it's a shuffle feel.

Rock Beat #17

Track 40

Even if you're playing mostly quarter-notes, you can slip some shuffle eighth-notes or triplets into the bass line. Here's an example of a walking bass line that you can play over the above beat.

Track 41

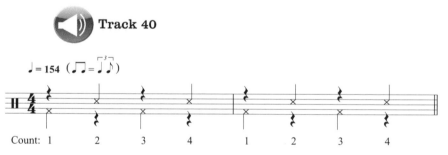

More Complex Beats

For more complex kick and snare patterns, identifying which drum hits are more prominent is essential to establishing the groove and outlining the chord progression. Let's start out with an easy one. The following drum beat contains the familiar syncopation that's emphasized by the kick drum occurring on beat 2 1/2.

Rock Beat #18

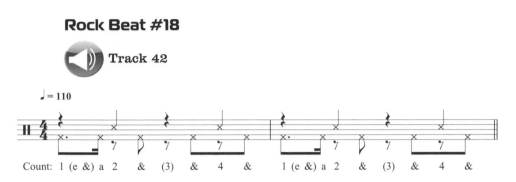

Count: 1 (e &) a 2 & (3) & 4 & | 1 (e &) a 2 & (3) & 4 &

If we strip the beat down to its basics, we're left with the essential kick drum hits on beats 1 and 2 1/2. Here's the simplified version:

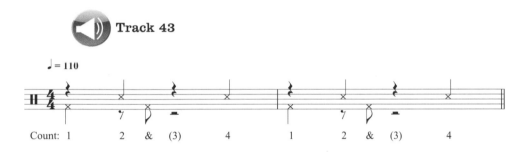

Count: 1 2 & (3) 4 | 1 2 & (3) 4

You'll find that it isn't necessary to play bass notes on every kick drum; you can still lock down the groove by playing on the main, emphasized beats. Here's an example using the original beat, but the bass only plays on the main kick drums occurring at beats 1 and 2 1/2.

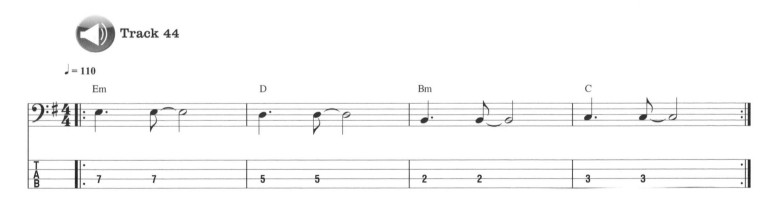

From the above example, you can see that there's no need to mirror the exact drum pattern with your bass. In fact, doing so can sometimes sound sterile and boring. By anchoring your bass line to the essential, accented beats, you can still lock in and do your own thing while the drummer does his. Allow the groove to breathe and concentrate on the feel and the flow of the beat. Once you have a grasp of the basic rhythm, you'll find it easier to add in a few more notes without clashing with the drums.

Here's a rhythmically similar example that changes chords on each of the accented beats.

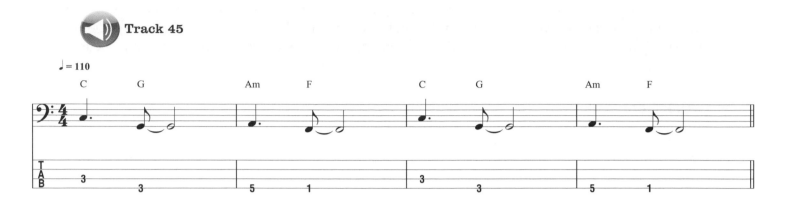

Track 45

Now let's go back to the previous bass line in E minor and add a few select notes that connect with the more complex drum pattern. Notice how simple it is to outline and maintain the basic groove. This is a concept we'll explore in more detail in upcoming chapters.

Track 46

This next beat contains some kick-drum syncopation and adds an extra snare drum hit on beat 3 1/4. Beats like this are common in grunge and modern rock songs from the 1990s.

Rock Beat #19

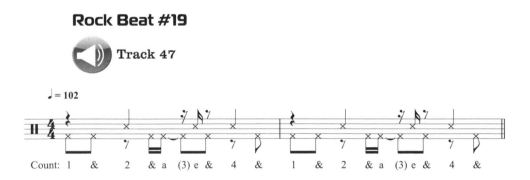

Track 47

Putting a solid bass line to the above beat is easy when you play along with the overall syncopated rhythmic pattern. The following example sticks to mostly root notes but incorporates a few additional chord tones to keep it interesting.

Track 48

This next beat is a slight variation of the previous one. The only difference is we've moved one of the kick drums from beat 3 1/2 to beat 3 3/4.

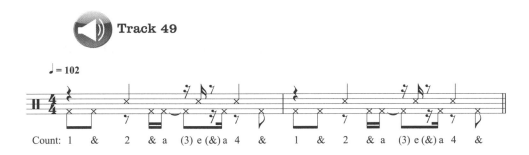

Track 49

Even though there's only a slight variation in the drum beat, we can change the groove dramatically with the bass by altering which beats the root notes are played on. Here are a few examples.

Track 50

Track 51

This next beat is a sort of reverse four-on-the-floor style beat. The snare drum plays on every downbeat while the bass drum plays around it. This beat is used in upbeat rock and pop styles and can be most notably heard in The Pretenders' song "Mystery Achievement."

Rock Beat #20

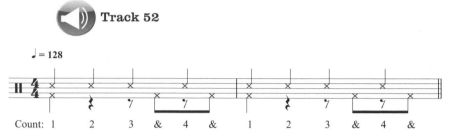

For the bass line, let's stay solid and sharp on the downbeats by hitting staccato quarter notes on beats 1 and 2. For the second half of the measure, we can add in some notes to follow the upbeat kick drums. In cases like this, it's possible that the bass riff was created first, and then the drummer attached this beat to enhance it.

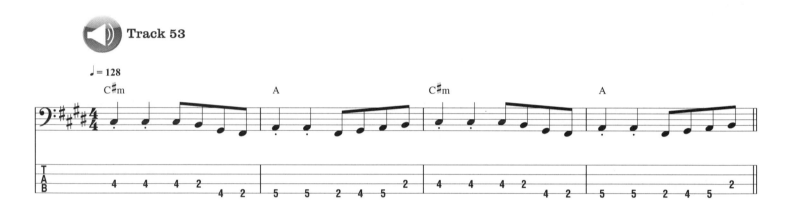

If we speed up the tempo of the previous beat and add kick drums to all of the upbeats, we'll come up with a pretty standard punk-style beat.

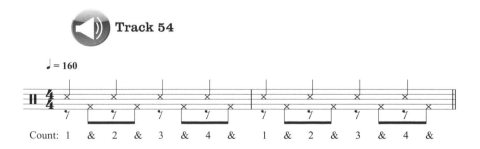

In cases like this, a good choice for the bass is to play aggressive eighth notes, making sure to give lots of emphasis to the downbeats. The next example is a pretty straightforward punk-style bass line that can be played along with the above drum beat.

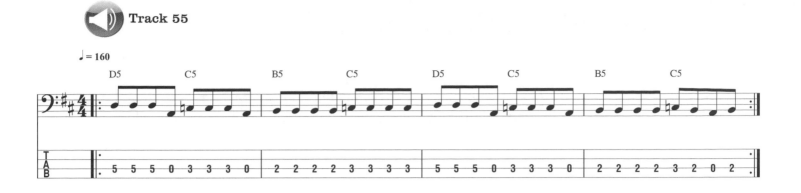

Lastly, here's a variation of the earlier 6/8 drum beat with some extra snare hits and a busier kick drum pattern.

Rock Beat #21

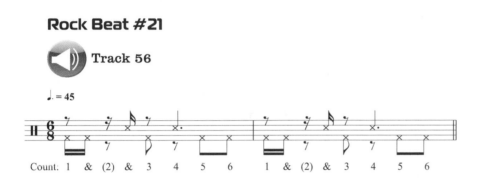

This bass line in 6/8 locks in with the above drum beat and uses a combination of chord tones and scale tones in the key of A minor. We'll expand on this approach in the upcoming chapters.

The beats explored in this chapter represent some of the most popular, basic drum patterns used in rock. There are countless other variations and styles that we haven't explored here. The main goal of this section was to get you used to listening to kick and snare drum patterns and to always pay attention to what the drummer is doing while you're playing. There's a popular saying that a band is only as good as their drummer. A great drummer will always make the bassist play and sound better, and vice versa.

PENTATONIC SCALE RIFFS

Pentatonic scales are the most popular scales in rock and blues music. Many bass lines and riffs are based on pentatonic scales, and countless bass players use them exclusively to improvise bass lines. A pentatonic scale is a five-note scale ("penta" means five).

The A Minor Pentatonic Scale

The minor pentatonic scale appears in the main riff of many popular songs, such as Aerosmith's "Toys in the Attic," Michael Jackson's "Billie Jean," and one of the most famous examples, Cream's "Sunshine of Your Love." Most riff-based songs are written using the minor pentatonic scale, but it's also the most common, go-to scale for bass players to use for fills and riffs. Many players use the minor pentatonic scale or variations of it for most of their bass parts.

Let's start out with one of the most useful keys: A minor. The scale diagram below shows one octave of the A minor pentatonic scale, starting at the fifth fret on the fourth string. The root notes, A, are indicated using white circles; the other notes are indicated using black circles.

A Minor Pentatonic

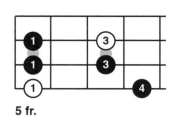

5 fr.

Here's the A minor pentatonic scale played in groups of three—first ascending, then descending. This is a popular scale pattern that will help get you comfortable using the scale for riffs and improvisation. You can apply this pattern when practicing other scales as well.

Track 58

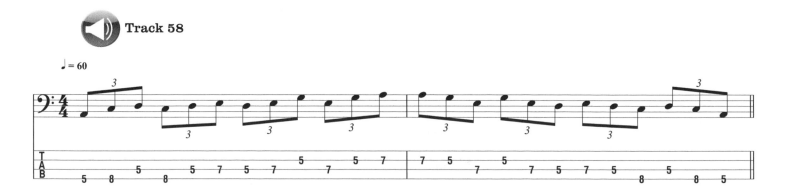

Here's an example of a rock bass line that uses the complete A minor pentatonic scale.

Track 59

$\downarrow = 120$

This next riff-based line incorporates syncopation while descending the scale.

Track 60

$\downarrow = 108$

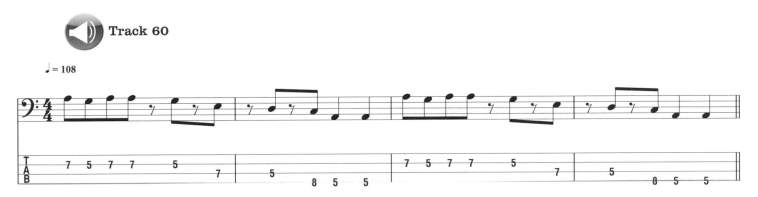

The following example uses a shuffle feel and triplets to create a hard rock bass line. It contains some hammer-ons and pull-offs in measures 2 and 4. These are useful techniques for playing riffs.

Track 61

$\downarrow = 96$

This next riff features some grace-note hammer-ons. This technique is very common when playing bass fills.

Track 62

$\downarrow = 108$

Since there are five different notes in the pentatonic scale, there are five distinct scale patterns (positions), each beginning on a different note of the scale. The first position starts with the first (root) degree of the scale, the second position begins on the second, and so on. Here are the five different scale positions for the A minor pentatonic scale, beginning with the first-position pattern, played at the fifth fret. Each pattern is shown ascending and descending in notation and tab.

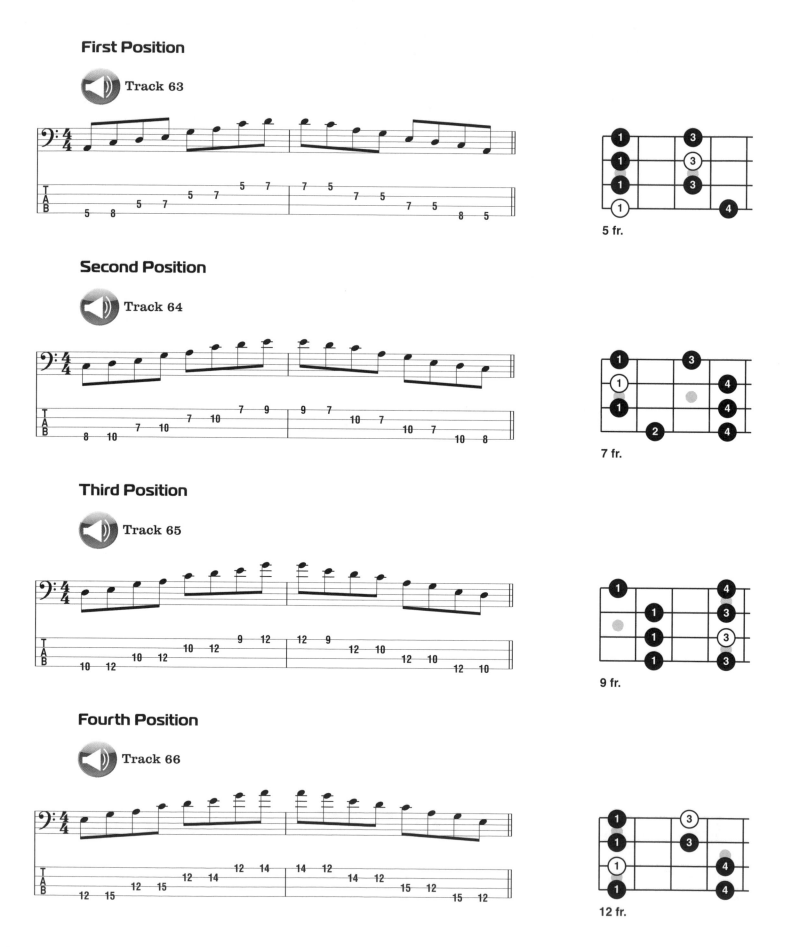

First Position

Track 63

Second Position

Track 64

Third Position

Track 65

Fourth Position

Track 66

Fifth Position

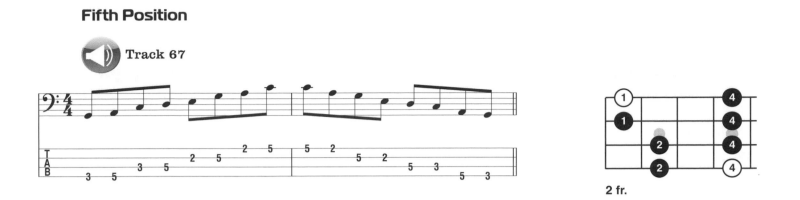

Track 67

Depending on the context, you can use alternate fingerings to make a few of these positions more comfortable to play. When playing the third-position scale pattern, for example, you can slightly pivot your hand position by substituting your fourth finger on the second string. Try the following fingering both ascending and descending:

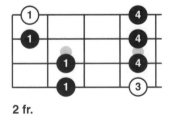

9 fr.

All of these fingerings are suggestions, and you should go with what feels most comfortable to you. Of course, it isn't necessary to use the altered fingering unless you're moving between the first and second strings. Similarly, we can alter the fifth-position scale like this:

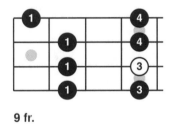

2 fr.

To give you a better sense of how these scale patterns overlap and span the entire fretboard, here's a complete fretboard diagram with the positions indicated using brackets. Again, all of the root notes are indicated with white circles.

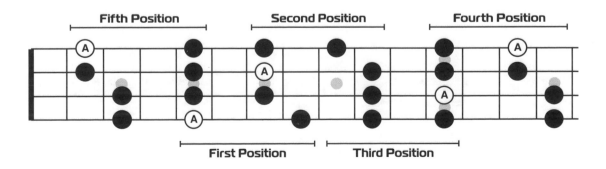

Once you've got command of the notes, it's easy to come up with pentatonic bass lines. Here's an example that uses a small part of the fifth-position A minor pentatonic scale.

Here's a bass line built on the third-position A minor pentatonic scale.

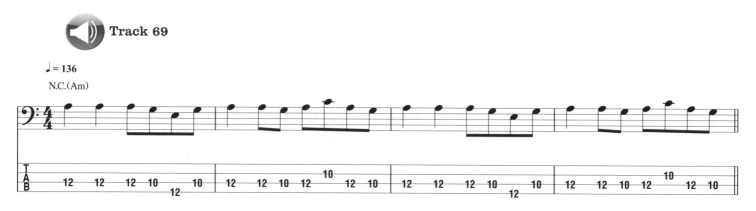

You can also combine multiple positions for effect and playability. This next riff starts out in the fifth position and then uses a grace-note slide to move up to the first position.

This next example is a pentatonic bass line played against a chord progression in A minor.

The E Minor Pentatonic Scale

The minor pentatonic scale positions can be transposed to any other key by moving the scale patterns up or down the fretboard. This is why it's essential to memorize where the root notes of the scale are in all of the scale positions. Here are all of the scale positions in the key of E minor, another commonly used key in rock. Play the root notes before and after each scale position, as shown in the notation and tab. This is a good exercise to apply to all of your scales, as it will improve your ability to use the scales in practical applications.

First Position

Second Position

Third Position

Fourth Position

Fifth Position

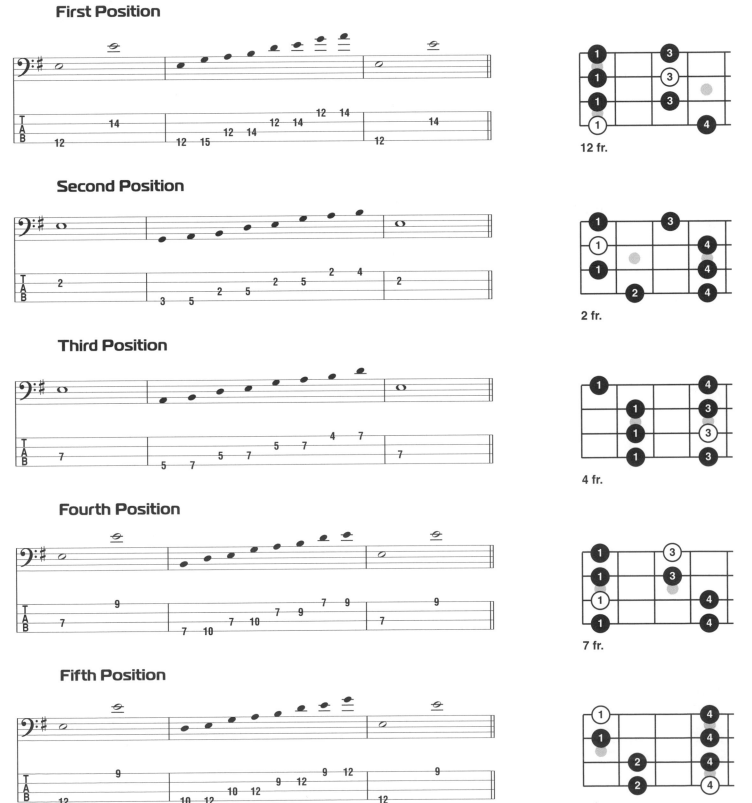

Now let's transpose the first-position E minor pentatonic scale pattern one octave lower to the open position. There are two different scale diagram fingerings presented on the right; both are useful for different applications. Fret the notes with your second and third fingers in situations where you might be incorporating chromatic passing tones at the first fret. Fret the notes with your first and second fingers to achieve greater speed and control when playing the "pure" pentatonic scale.

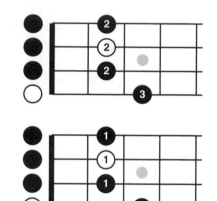

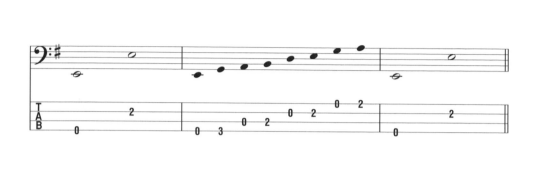

The following E minor pentatonic riff is based around the third-position scale pattern and incorporates some of the notes from the open position scale. Many rock bass riffs using E minor pentatonic use this approach, playing mainly around the fifth and seventh frets while using the low open E for the root.

🔊 **Track 72**

This next example uses the fourth-position E minor pentatonic scale. The rhythm is a moderate walking bass in a shuffle feel, similar to the riff from "Money" by Pink Floyd.

🔊 **Track 73**

Now let's put the E minor pentatonic scale into a real song application. This example uses a popular chord progression in the key of E minor: Em–C–D–Em. We'll start off by playing the groove using just the root notes and then we'll gradually add pentatonic riffs to the fourth measure of the progression. As the bass line gets busier, we can add some pentatonic riffs to the first and third measures as well. You'll notice that there are no riffs against the C chord. Since the note C is not present in the E minor pentatonic scale, it's best to use other note choices to improvise against the C chord, such as arpeggios or passing tones, both of which are techniques that we'll explore in upcoming chapters.

Track 74

The above bass line may seem a little busy, and this may not be the best approach to use when playing a verse or chorus where you might clash with the vocals. However, improvised lines like this are common for backing up a guitar solo or jamming during an outro.

The A Major Pentatonic Scale

Scales that contain the same notes are called *relative scales*. Each major scale has a relative minor scale, and vice versa. Since you already know all of the scale patterns for the minor pentatonic scale, the following major pentatonic scales will look familiar; however, since they are now in a major key, the placement of the root notes in each position is different. Here are the five scale patterns for the A major pentatonic scale, starting with the first-position pattern, beginning on the root note, A, at the fifth fret of the fourth string. Play through the patterns as shown, playing the root notes in each position both before and after the scale pattern.

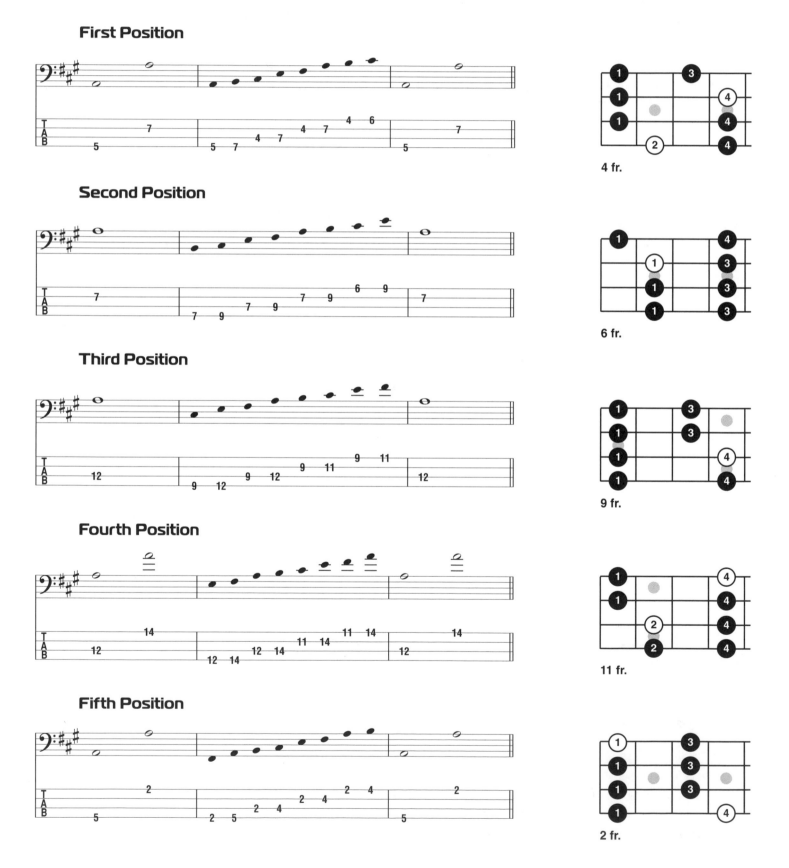

First Position

Second Position

Third Position

Fourth Position

Fifth Position

Here's a traditional bass line using the first position of the A major pentatonic scale.

Track 75

Here's another old-school rock bass line that uses the notes of the second-position major pentatonic.

Track 76

This next example weaves a bass riff across the first three scale positions by utilizing grace-note slides. Notice that the entire riff can be fretted using just your first and third fingers.

Track 77

The examples in this chapter were created to give you a basic background and understanding of how to apply the major and minor pentatonic scales. Once you've got the scale positions mastered and can transpose them to any key, you'll be able to visualize the scale across the entire fretboard. The pentatonics are the arguably the most important scales you'll use to create rock bass lines and riffs. At this point, you'll likely recognize these scale patterns in plenty of classic songs you may already know. Remember, many professional players have practically based an entire career on just these scales, so you'll encounter them in countless songs and styles.

ROCK CHORD PROGRESSIONS

Most rock songs are comprised of a series of chords played in a specific order called a *chord progression*. In this chapter, we'll explore some of the most popular chord progressions and show you how to identify them in any key. Learning the basic theory behind these progressions will help demystify song structure and lay the groundwork you'll use for creating your own bass lines.

Chord Theory

The basic chords in a musical key are created by starting with any specific note in the scale and then stacking every other note of the scale on top of it. For example, using the first note of the C major scale (C), we can add the third note (E) and the fifth note (G) of the scale. This will give us the notes of a C major triad: C–E–G (R–3–5). In this fashion, we can build a chord on every step of the scale. Some chords will be major and some will be minor, depending on which step of the scale the chord is built on. This is true for every major key.

In order to figure out the order of the chords for each key, we use Roman numerals. Uppercase Roman numerals refer to major chords, while lowercase Roman numerals refer to minor chords. The 3rd of each chord determines whether it's major or minor. If we use triads (three-note chords) exclusively, all of the chords will be major or minor in quality, with the only exception being the chord built on the seventh step of the scale. This is a diminished chord because it contains a diminished (flatted) 5th.

Here are all of the basic, three-note chords in the key of C major. The Roman numeral analysis can be applied to any other major key, and the order and quality of the chords remains the same—the I chord is always major, the ii chord is always minor, and so on.

I	ii	iii	IV	V	vi	vii°
C	Dm	Em	F	G	Am	B°
major	minor	minor	major	major	minor	diminshed

Now let's transpose the chords to another key: A major. As you can see, the order of the major and minor chords is exactly the same.

I	ii	iii	IV	V	vi	vii°
A	B	C♯	D	E	F♯	G♯°
major	minor	minor	major	major	minor	diminshed

You can also build chords in minor keys by harmonizing the minor scale. Here are the chords in the key of A minor.

i	ii°	III	iv	v	VI	VII
Am	B°	C	Dm	Em	F	G
minor	diminshed	major	minor	minor	major	major

Here is the order of the chords in major and minor keys, shown with only Roman numerals:

Major Keys

major	minor	minor	major	major	minor	diminshed
I	ii	iii	IV	V	vi	vii°

Minor Keys

minor	diminshed	major	minor	minor	major	major
i	ii°	III	iv	v	VI	VII

Major Progressions

Now let's take a look at some of the most popular chord progressions in major keys.

I–IV–V

The I–IV–V progression is a classic that's been used since the early days of rock music, and it's still used in many songs today. Most blues songs are based on a I–IV–V progression. Here's an example in the key of C major, with the bass sticking to the root notes and playing an eighth-note rhythm.

Track 78

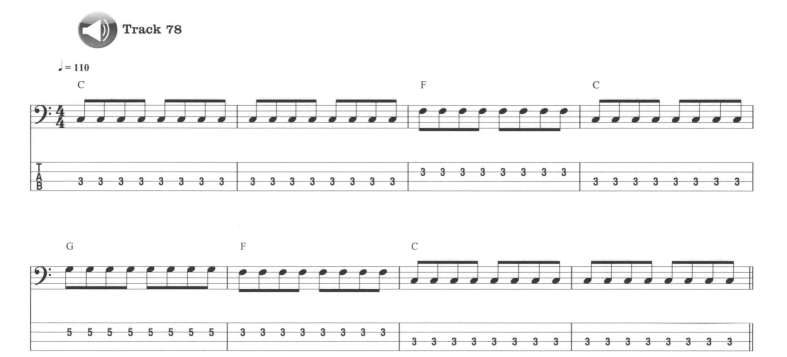

For this next example, let's transpose the I–IV–V progression to the key of G major. The bass line uses the notes of the major pentatonic scale for each chord to create a popular, riff-based line that's reminiscent of early surf-rock music.

Track 79

It's not unusual to switch up the progression a little, both rhythmically and with the order and duration of the chords. Here's an example in the key of D major.

Track 80

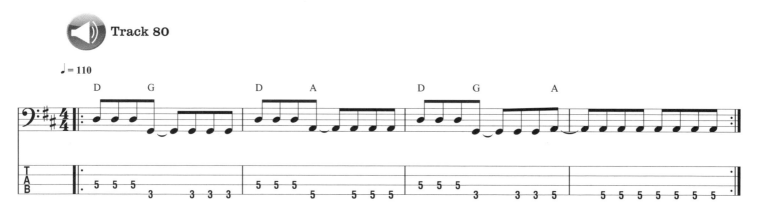

Here's a rock example in E major that also includes the minor 3rd (the note G) from the minor pentatonic scale to give the progression a heavier sound. This is reminiscent of the Joan Jett song, "I Love Rock 'n' Roll."

Track 81

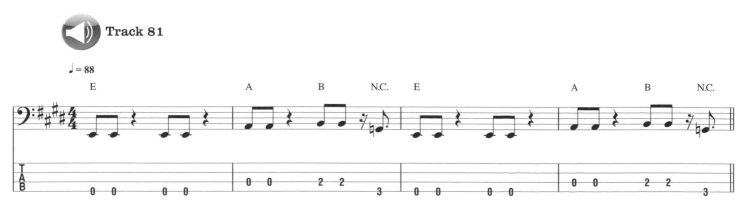

I–♭VII–IV

Here's another popular three-chord progression that's often used in major keys: I–♭VII–IV. By lowering the root of the seventh chord one half step, it becomes a major chord. On the fretboard, this progression looks a lot like the I–IV–V progression. It's basically taking the I, IV, and V chords and switching the order around so that in context, the V chord now functions as the root (I chord). The following example is a I–♭VII–IV progression in the key of A major.

Track 82

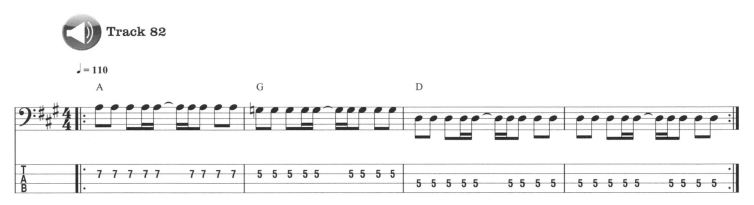

Here's the same progression transposed to E major. Notice that this example starts on the low E for the I chord and then jumps up to the D at the fifth fret for the ♭VII chord. The progression is still the same as the previous example, even though the root notes of the chords are played in different octaves. This is why the ability to identify the progression by Roman numeral analysis is important.

Track 83

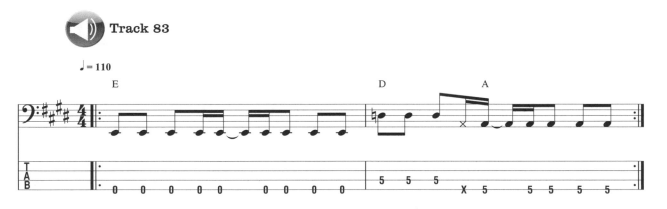

I–V–vi–IV

This four-chord progression is one of the most commonly used major-key progressions in modern rock and pop music. You'll recognize this progression from thousands of popular songs, so it's important for you to be able to play it in different keys and with the root notes played in different octaves. In later chapters, we'll revisit this progression to show you how to add melody to your bass lines. This first example is in the key of C major.

Track 84

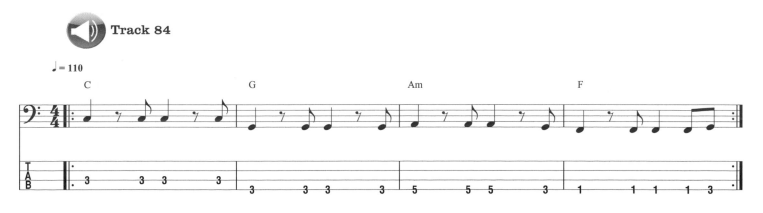

Here's another example of the I–V–vi–IV progression. This one is in 6/8 time in the key of F major, with the root of the I chord (F) as the lowest note in the bass line.

Track 85

This next example features the chords of the I–V–vi–IV in the key of D major. Instead of playing each chord for a full measure as in the previous two bass lines, this example mixes up the rhythm and returns to the V chord at the end of the progression.

Track 86

IV–I–V–vi

This popular progression is a slight variation of the previous one. It uses the same chords in the same order, but the progression starts on the IV chord instead of the I chord. This example is in the key of A major, with the bass playing low E and low F♯ for V and vi chords, respectively.

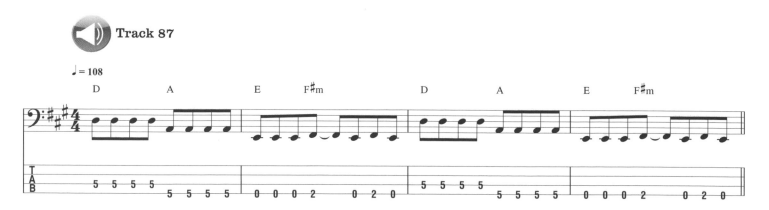

Track 87

I–V–vi

Here's a three-chord variation of the previous progression that leaves off the IV chord entirely. The following bass line—also in A major—is similar to "Jailbreak" by Thin Lizzy.

Track 88

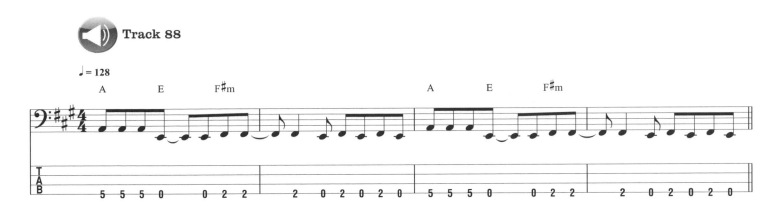

I–V–ii–IV

This progression is also similar to the I–V–vi–IV progression; we've simply substituted the ii chord for the vi chord. Here's the progression in the key of G major.

Track 89

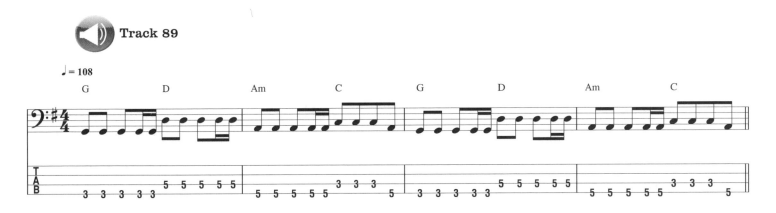

I–V–iii–IV

Now let's take the above progression and substitute the iii chord for the ii chord. This is a popular move in modern rock songs from the '90s.

Track 90

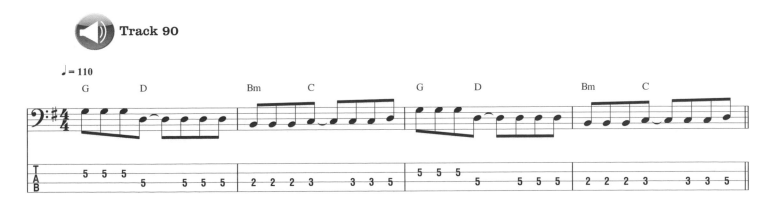

Minor Progressions

Every major key has a specific *relative minor* key (and vice-versa) that contains all of the same notes and key signature. The minor scale is built on the sixth step of its relative major scale. For example, the sixth step of the C major scale is the note A, so if you play the notes of the C major scale from A to the A one octave higher, you'll have an A minor scale. Conversely, the major scale is built on the third step of its relative minor scale.

Let's explore some of the popular chord progressions in minor keys. At this point, you'll probably begin to recognize familiar patterns in the order of which the chords are arranged. Some of these minor progressions will use the same chords as the major progressions, however, the tonic (i chord) is what establishes the minor key and determines the Roman numeral analysis.

The following chart shows all of the chords in the key of A minor, with the chords in the relative key of C major below them. Notice that both keys contain all of the same chords. The chord that functions as the tonic (i chord or I chord) is what establishes the key and tonal center.

i	ii°	III	iv	v	VI	VII		
Am	B°	C	Dm	Em	F	G		
minor	diminshed	major	minor	minor	major	major		
		I	ii	iii	IV	V	vi	vii°
		C	Dm	Em	F	G	Am	B°
		major	minor	minor	major	major	minor	diminshed

i–VI–VII–i

Our first minor progression is the most popular, go-to chord progression used in many heavy metal and hard rock songs. Here it is in the key of A minor played over a typical rock beat.

🔊 **Track 91**

This next example features the same i–VI–VII–i progression in the key of E minor, using a popular heavy metal rhythm reminiscent of many songs by Iron Maiden. This progression was also used in the previous chapter to demonstrate minor pentatonic scale riffs.

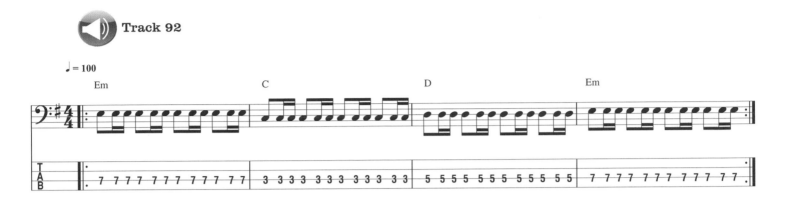

Track 92

i–VI

Many rock songs will simplify the above progression by using just the i and VI chords. Here's an example in E minor.

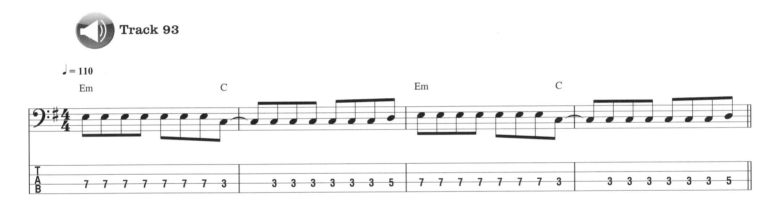

Track 93

A lot of the examples in this section will be shown in the popular key of E minor, making it easier for you to compare the progressions and recognize their differences. E minor is often used in rock in order to utilize the low open E string for the tonic. Here's the previous progression played in F♯ minor, which is another popular minor key.

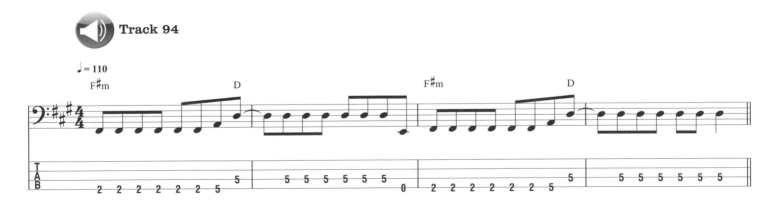

Track 94

i–VI–VII–v

Here's another variation of the previous progression that introduces a minor v chord into the mix.

Track 95

i–VII–VI–V

Sometimes it's preferable to alter the minor v chord to make it a major V chord instead. This is a common practice that was co-opted from early classical music when chords in minor keys were often built on a *harmonic minor scale* (a minor scale with a raised seventh). This particular progression can be heard in the chorus of "N.I.B." by Black Sabbath.

Track 96

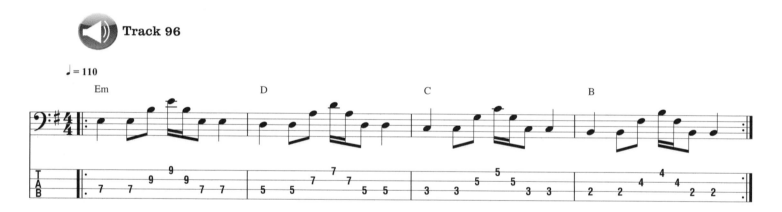

i–VI–iv–VII

This progression is a variation of the i–VI–VII that inserts a minor iv chord into the mix.

Track 97

i–VI–III–VII

The use of the major III chord is also common in minor-key progressions. This progression is the same as the previous one, except that we've substituted the iv chord (Am) with the III chord (G).

Track 98

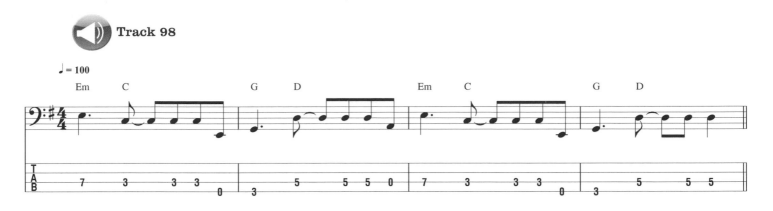

i–VII–III–VI

The previous progression works just as well if you switch the order of the chords around. In this case, we've opted to play the note G an octave higher in the bass line.

Track 99

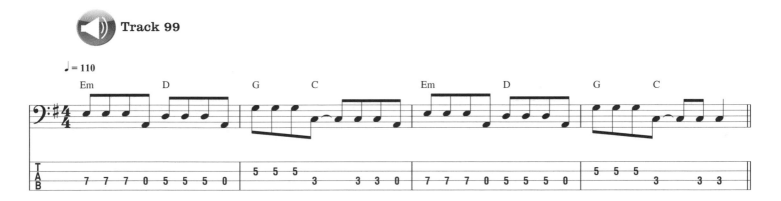

i–III–VII–VI

Let's vary the order of the chords again, this time placing the III chord (G) second in the progression.

Track 100

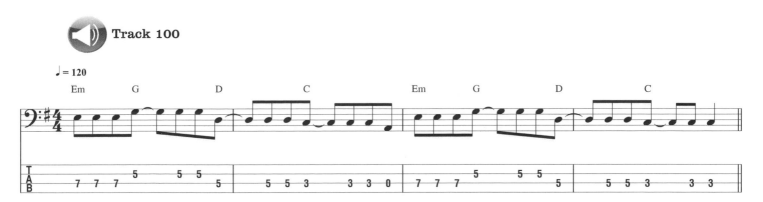

i–III–VII–iv

Let's take the previous progression and substitute the VI chord (C) with the iv chord (Am). To make things a little more interesting, we've thrown in some scale tones to show you how a bass melody will work against this progression. When each chord in the progression changes, the bass plays the root note of the chord, anchoring the harmonic structure within the melody. We'll explore this approach in detail in the coming chapters.

Track 101

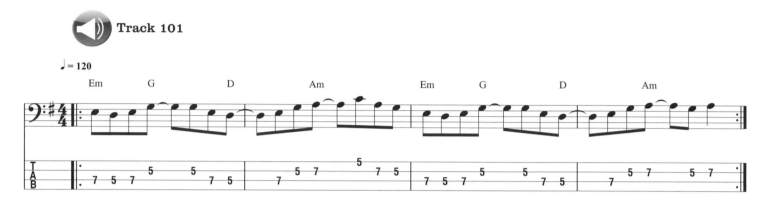

Longer Chord Progressions

Up until this point, we've focused on shorter progressions that only use three or four chords. While those progressions are more common in mainstream rock and popular music, it's possible to string together longer progressions that utilize more chords. The following example in the key of A minor is played in 6/8 and uses five different chords. This 16-bar progression can easily represent a full verse of a song. Notice that we're using the major V chord (E) instead of the minor version of the chord.

Track 102

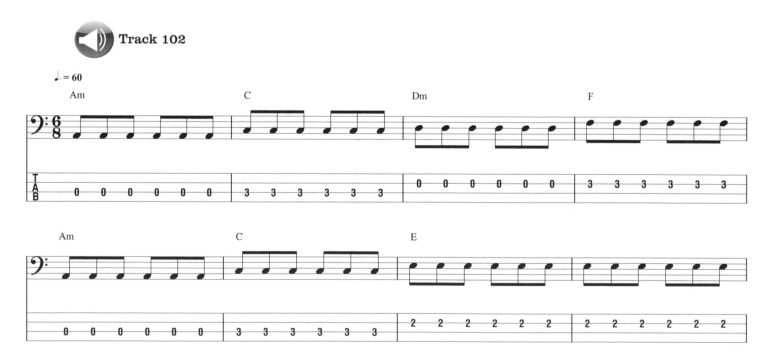

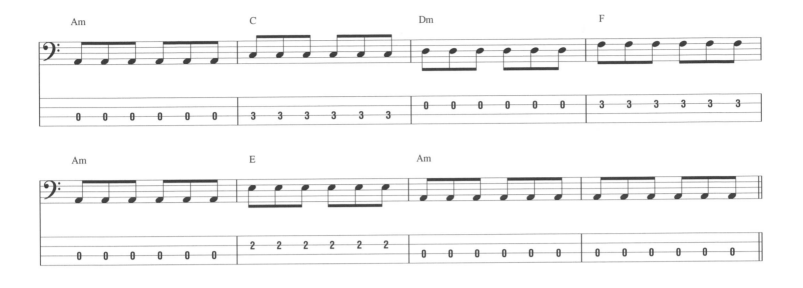

Here's a classically influenced progression that can be heard in the outro-solo of Ozzy Osbourne's "Mr. Crowley." The diminished ii chord (E°) is used here, as well as the altered major V chord (A).

Track 103

♩ = 102

> *Memorizing popular chord progressions by their Roman numeral analysis will enable you to create bass lines against them in any key. We've explored some of the most commonly used progressions in this chapter, but there are numerous variations and chord alterations that can be applied to make them unique and interesting. We'll encounter more complex chord progressions in upcoming chapters and show you how to use arpeggios and scales to seamlessly weave your bass lines into melodic masterpieces. Your command of the chord progressions will help you to construct great bass lines and also expand your musical vocabulary, enabling you to write your own songs.*

An *arpeggio* is defined as the notes of a chord played separately. For example, a C major chord is made up of three notes: C, E, and G. If you play those three notes individually on the bass, you're playing a C major arpeggio. Knowing your arpeggios and being adept at playing them is invaluable to the bass player because they represent the notes of the chords being played by the rest of the band and will be among the best note choices when constructing bass lines.

The Major Arpeggio

Let's start out with a basic C major arpeggio, consisting of the notes C, E, and G. Notice that these notes are the first, third, and fifth notes of the C major scale and are usually referred to in musical terms as the root, 3rd, and 5th. For practical purposes, we can also add the octave C (the "eighth" step of the major scale). The most comfortable way to play the major arpeggio is to start out with your second finger on the root note, as shown below in the fretboard diagram. The root note and the octave, C, are indicated with white circles; the other notes are indicated with black circles.

C Major Arpeggio

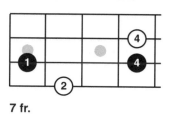

7 fr.

Here's an example of a simple bass line using major arpeggios against a variation of the I–IV–V chord change in the key of A major.

🔊 **Track 104**

In most cases, you probably won't be using all of the notes of the arpeggios in succession as shown above. Remember that these notes are all present in the chords being played, so they represent go-to notes that will fit into your bass lines. The most popular note choice for bass players (outside of the root note and the octave) is the 5th, and you'll see it constantly used in bass lines. You really can't go wrong with the 5th, since the interval is the same whether the chord is major or minor. Let's set aside the 3rd for now and take a look at some examples using only 5ths and octaves.

Here's an example of a popular bass groove using root notes and 5ths.

Track 105

Another common move for bass players is to transpose the 5th an octave lower and play it beneath the root note instead of above it. Notice how the example below sticks to the root notes on the downbeats and uses the 5th sparingly on the upbeats.

Track 106

Before we get back to incorporating the 3rds, let's take a look at one example using 5ths and octaves together. This is a pretty popular move that's used by everyone from Steve Harris to Geezer Butler to James Jamerson. It sounds impressive, especially when played at a faster tempo, but once you have command of the 5ths and octaves, you can easily pull off lines like this.

Track 107

Here's a basic McCartney-esque line in the key of A major that demonstrates the strict use of major arpeggios on each chord. In the seventh measure, the 3rd and 5th of the D major arpeggio are played an octave lower, below the root note.

Track 108

This next example is a surf-rock bass line using a I–IV–V progression in A major. To make arpeggio lines a bit more interesting, it's common to add extra notes as shown here. In this case, the 6th is added to each arpeggio.

Track 109

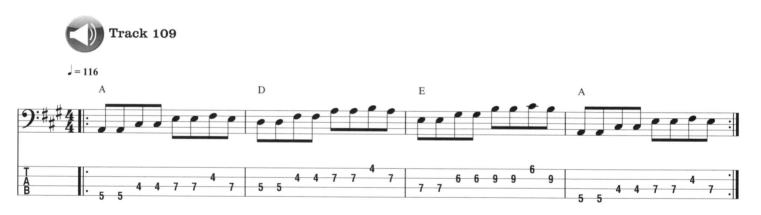

The Minor Arpeggio

Now let's take a look at the A minor arpeggio, consisting of the notes A, C, and E—the first, third, and fifth notes of the A minor scale. For practical purposes, we can also add the octave A (the eighth step of the A minor scale). The most comfortable way to play the minor arpeggio is to start out with your first finger on the root note.

A Minor Arpeggio

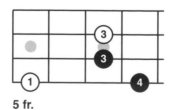

5 fr.

The distance between the root note and the 5th is the same for both the major and minor arpeggios; what differentiates them is the 3rd. In a major arpeggio, the distance from the root note to the 3rd is two whole steps, or a *major 3rd*; in a minor arpeggio, the distance is one-and-a-half steps, or a *minor 3rd*.

Here's an example in the key of E minor that uses the E minor arpeggio in the context of a i–VI–VII progression.

 Track 110

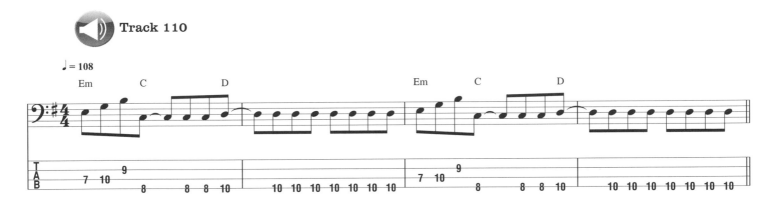

Remember, it's not necessary to use all of the notes of the arpeggio. In the example below, we'll just use the root and the 3rd of the E minor arpeggio for our bass line. Notice that these notes are the first two notes of the E minor pentatonic scale as well.

Track 111

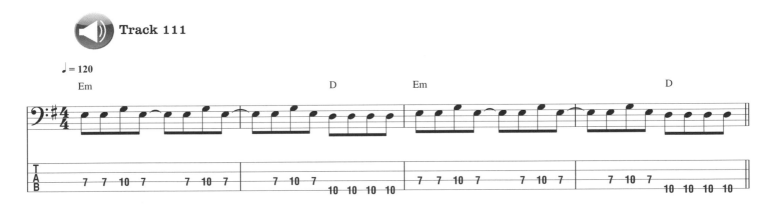

Alternate Fingerings

It's a good idea to learn some other ways to play the arpeggios in addition to the basic fingerings we've covered so far. Here are a few alternate fingerings for the major and minor arpeggios; both require significant five-fret stretches. The major arpeggio starts with your first finger on the root note; the minor arpeggio starts with your second finger on the root note.

C Major Arpeggio

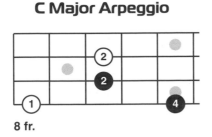

8 fr.

A Minor Arpeggio

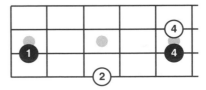

3 fr.

Here are a few more fingerings for the major and minor arpeggios, both starting with your fourth finger on the root notes:

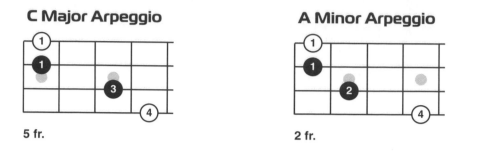

C Major Arpeggio

5 fr.

A Minor Arpeggio

2 fr.

Using the Major and Minor Arpeggios

Here are some bass lines that use both the major and minor arpeggios. This first example is in the key of E minor.

Track 112

This next example in the key of D major features a I–V–ii–IV chord progression. There are some interesting things about this bass line that we can point out. Notice that the 5th of the D major arpeggio is the note A, which is also the root note of the next chord, A major. This same phenomenon occurs with the A major arpeggio in the second measure as well; the 5th of the A major arpeggio is the note E, which is also the root note of the following chord, Em. These are perfect examples of how to use the arpeggios to create seamless bass lines that connect the chords in the progression. In addition, the minor 3rd of the E minor arpeggio is the note G, which is the root note of the following chord, G major.

Track 113

You can also create chord *inversions* by playing the 3rd or the 5th of the arpeggio in the bass, instead of playing the root note. The following example shows a simple chord progression twice so you can hear the difference. The first time, the bass plays all root notes; the second time, the bass plays the 3rd for a few of the chords. Inversions are indicated in the chord analysis above the staff using slashed chord symbols. For example, the chord symbol D/F♯ indicates that the chord is D major, but the bass is playing F♯ (the 3rd of the D major chord).

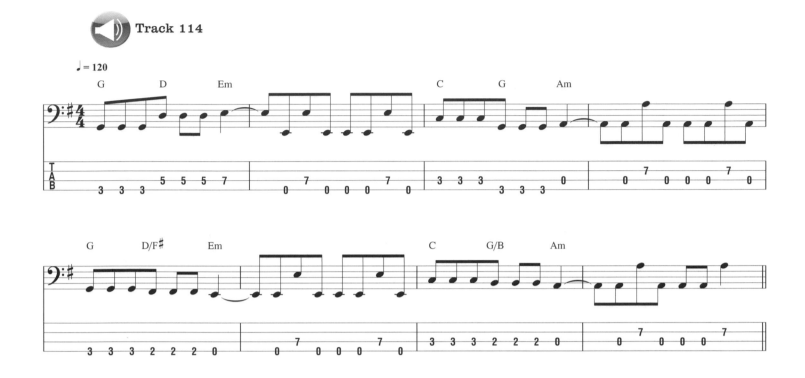

Seventh-Chord Arpeggios

If we extend each of the arpeggios one more chord tone, we get seventh chords. There are four main types of seventh chords: major seventh (maj7), minor seventh (m7), dominant seventh (7), and minor seventh flat-five (m7♭5). Here are the popular fingerings for the seventh-chord arpeggios, all shown using A at the fifth fret as the root note:

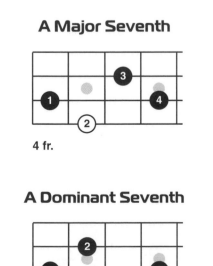

A Major Seventh

4 fr.

A Minor Seventh

5 fr.

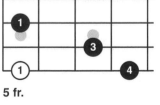

A Dominant Seventh

4 fr.

A Minor Seventh Flat-Five

5 fr.

The following example is based on a i–iv–v progression in the key of A minor and uses all minor seventh arpeggios. The bass repeats the same pattern for each chord. Notice how similar the minor seventh arpeggio is to the minor pentatonic scale; the arpeggio contains four of the pentatonic scale's five notes.

Track 115

This next example is a I–IV–V walking pattern using all dominant seventh chords. In addition to the notes of the arpeggio, we've added the 6th of each chord to the riff. This popular bass line should sound very familiar to you.

Track 116

We can harmonize the major scale using all seventh chords, the same way we previously harmonized the scale with triads. Each step of the major scale yields a specific seventh chord:

Here's an exercise that progresses through all of the seventh-chord arpeggios in the key of C major. It begins on the Cmaj7 arpeggio with the root note on the third string at the third fret and then moves up the fretboard one arpeggio at a time until it reaches the octave at the 15th fret. This exercise will help you memorize which arpeggio is used for each step of the major scale. In future chapters, we'll utilize these seventh-chord arpeggios in musical applications.

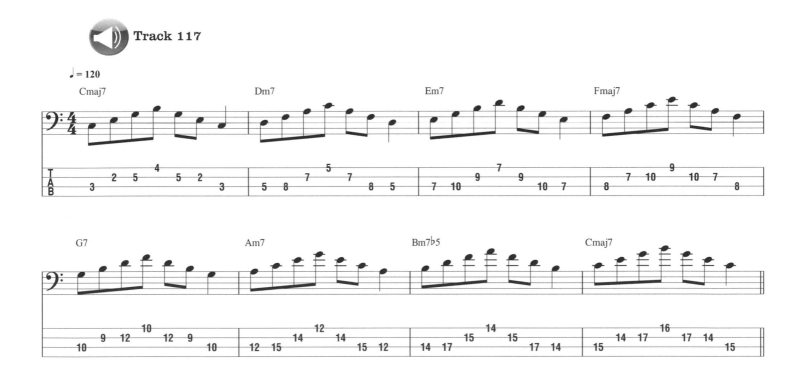

> *When learning the arpeggios, try not to get bogged down or intimidated by the theory. Most bassists and guitarists use pattern recognition to memorize arpeggios and scales. If you know where your root notes are, then you can visually find the 3rds and 5ths without worrying about all of the note names. Learning and memorizing every note on the bass is a gradual process that you'll master in time. Also, remember that the arpeggios are the notes of the chords played separately, so those notes represent good choices for your bass lines. It's not necessary to play the complete arpeggios all the time. Just remember to be aware of where your 3rds and 5ths are—both above and below the root note—and you'll be able to use them in more creative ways.*

ADDING MELODY

We've already explored the major and minor pentatonic scales, which are generally the most popular scales used by rock bass players, but you can explore the full melodic potential of the instrument by learning the complete major and minor scales. Navigating these scales, and knowing how to apply them to chord progressions, is admittedly more complicated than playing pentatonic riffs, but in this chapter, we'll try to strip away the mystery and get you started.

The C Major Scale

The major scale forms the foundation of most other scales and chords. If you count up from C to C in the musical alphabet (C–D–E–F–G–A–B–C), you'll have the C major scale. C major is unique in that it contains all natural notes (no sharps or flats). Here's one octave of the C major scale, starting at the third fret of the third string. The root notes, C, are circled in the notation and tab and are indicated with white dots in the scale diagram.

Track 118

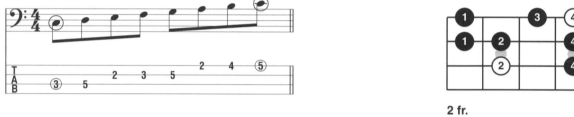

2 fr.

The notes of the major scale are separated by two different types of intervals—half steps (H) and whole steps (W). Natural half steps occur in the musical alphabet between the notes B and C, and E and F. With this knowledge, we can take a look at the C major scale and see that the half steps occur between the third and fourth, and seventh and eighth (octave) degrees of the scale. This information gives us the formula W–W–H–W–W–W–H for the major scale. All major scales, no matter the key, contain this same series of half steps and whole steps.

The following example shows how you can use the notes of the C major scale to create a melodic bass line against a I–V–vi–IV chord progression in the key of C major. For this bass line, we've used only the notes from the one-octave scale shown above.

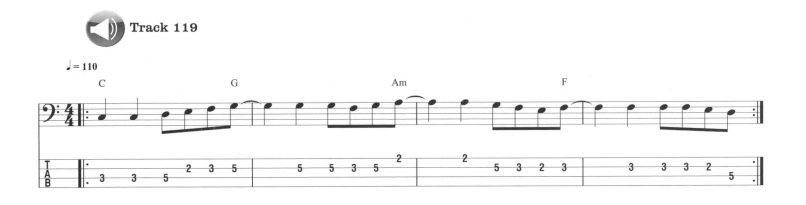

Track 119

The A Minor Scale

As we learned with the pentatonic scales, A minor is the relative key to C major. Therefore, the A minor scale contains the same notes as the C major scale (both keys contain only *natural notes*, no sharps or flats). As a rule, the relative minor scale begins on the 6th step of its relative major scale: the note A is the 6th step of the C major scale. This holds true for all relative keys.

Track 120

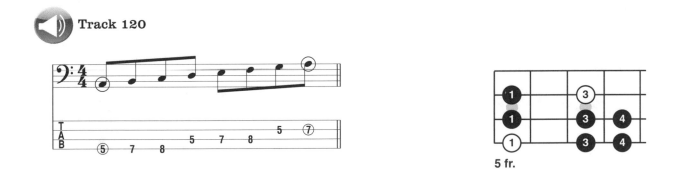

The minor scale yields its own unique order of half steps and whole steps (W–H–W–W–H–W–W) as shown in the diagram below.

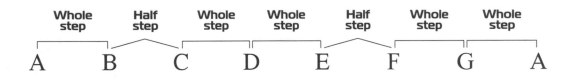

Here's an example of a bass line with a metal-style feel and chord progression. All of the notes come from the first-position A minor scale shown above.

Track 121

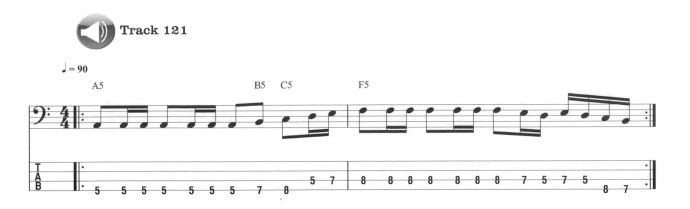

The Five Positions of the G Major Scale

There are five comfortable scale patterns that can be used to play the notes of the major scale across the entire fretboard. Each of the following five G major scale patterns contains all of the notes that are playable in G major in that area of the fretboard. As with the pentatonic scales, learn these scale patterns and memorize where the root notes are in each position. Once you've got them down, you can transpose them to other keys, enabling you to create major-scale bass lines in any key and position.

First Position

 Track 122

Second Position

Track 123

Third Position

Track 124

Fourth Position

Track 125

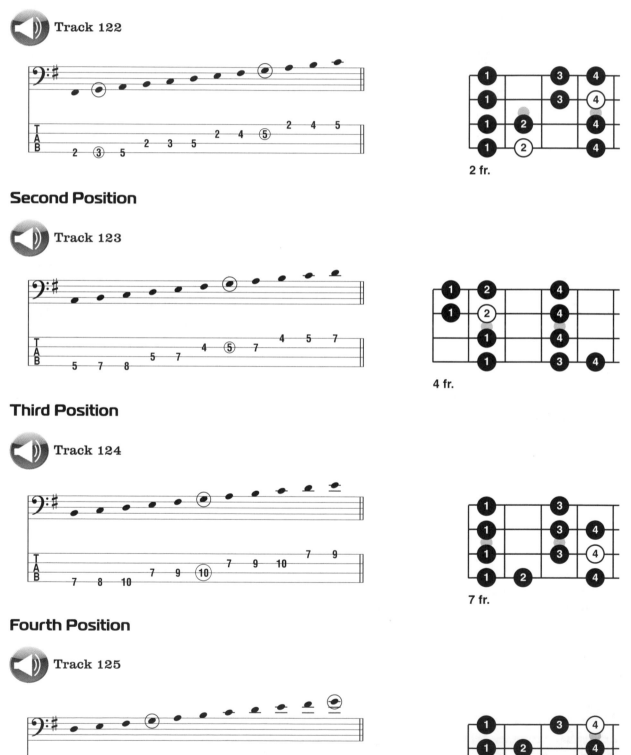

Fifth Position

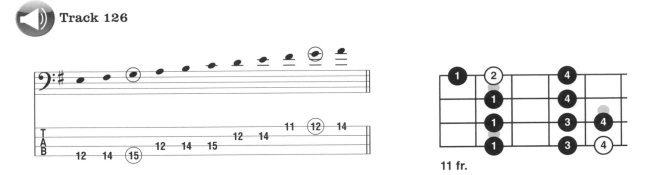

Track 126

Here's a bass line in G major played against a simple I–IV chord progression. The bass starts out in the third-position pattern, then moves up to the fourth-position pattern, ascending and descending different sections of the scale to melodically connect the chords.

Track 127

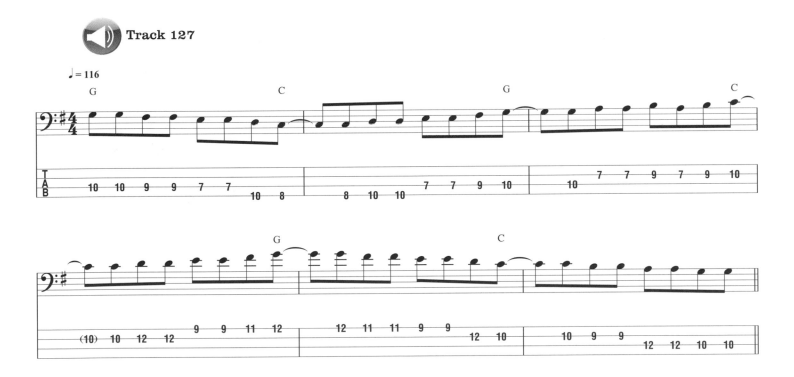

This next melodic example demonstrates how you can combine elements of the major scale and the major pentatonic scale. The bass line is spread out along the third and fourth strings; the slide lines indicate where to switch positions.

Track 128

Adding Melody 55

The Five Positions of the E Minor Scale

The E minor scale is the G major scale's relative minor, therefore both keys contain the same notes. The scale patterns are the same, but we've renumbered the positions so that the first position begins on the root note, and so on. As before, memorize where the root notes are in each position.

First Position

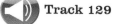 Track 129

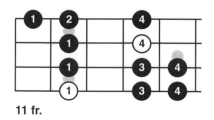

11 fr.

Second Position

Track 130

2 fr.

Third Position

Track 131

4 fr.

Fourth Position

Track 132

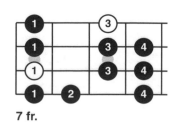

7 fr.

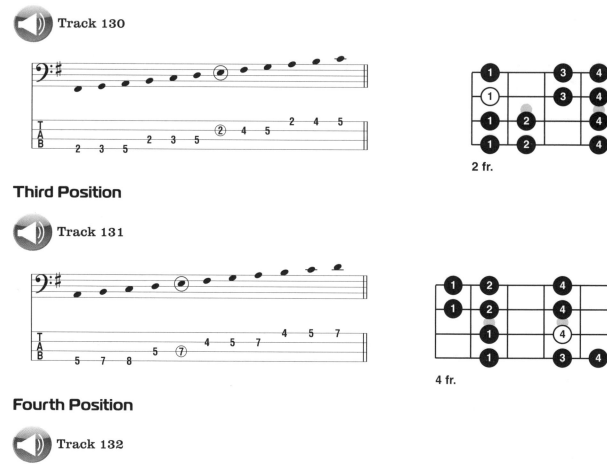

Fifth Position

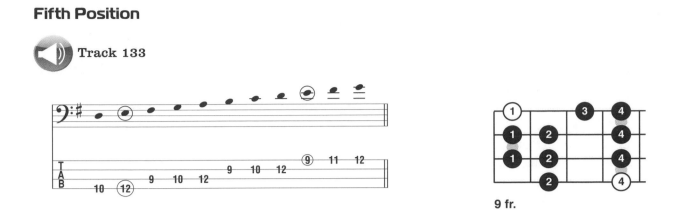

Track 133

Since E minor is a popular key, you'll want to play the scale in open position too. Here's the first-position scale pattern transposed one octave lower to open position.

First Position (Open Position)

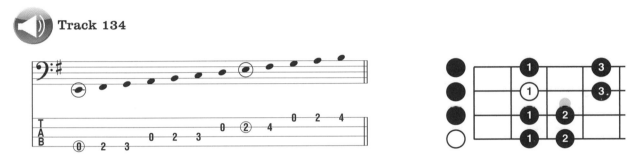

Track 134

The following example is a i–VI–III–VII chord progression in E minor. The bass line uses multiple positions of the E minor scale to connect the chords with melodic passages. The slide lines have been added as suggestions for where you can change scale positions.

Track 135

Melodic Approaches and Themes

The first half of this chapter explored the different positions of the major and minor scales along with a few simple examples of how to use them. Now let's apply these scales in a way that's a little more interesting. Given all of the information presented in this book, your ultimate goal is to combine the many elements of rhythm, harmony, and melody to create unique and effective bass lines. Remember that the main function of the bass is to hold down the bottom while contributing to the overall arrangement of the song. This can't be accomplished by simply playing up and down the scales, which isn't very creative and may also detract from the groove or step on the song's melody. Always listen to the vocals and other instruments in the band, and you'll be able to identify spots where you can drop in tasteful bass riffs and melodic passages that enhance the song.

The following example is a V–vi–IV–I progression in G major, with the emphasis on beats 1 and 2 1/2 in each measure. After establishing the groove and harmonic structure by playing root notes on those beats, we can add some melodic fills and passing tones to the rest of each measure.

Track 136

Here's an example featuring two chords per measure, giving you less space between the chords to work with. This is a two-measure i–VI–III–VII progression in the key of C♯ minor, played through twice. First let's play the example using just the root notes.

Track 137

Here's the same progression using the notes of the minor scale and the arpeggios to add melody to the bass line.

Track 138

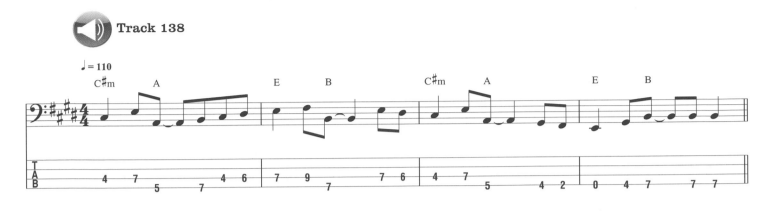

Another popular approach involves creating a melodic theme that repeats itself over each chord of the progression. The following I–ii–IV–I progression in G major demonstrates this in three different ways. We could analyze the relationship between the melodic notes and each chord, but that might be over-thinking it. As long as you're playing notes from the scale that sound as though they fit with each chord, you can use your ear to come up with tasteful lines like this.

Track 139

The next example takes advantage of available space to create a call-and-response effect in the bass line. The rhythm and chord change are outlined with staccato eighth notes on beat 1 of each measure. For the rest of each measure, the bass jumps up into the higher register and weaves a descending melodic theme that fits perfectly with the changing chords.

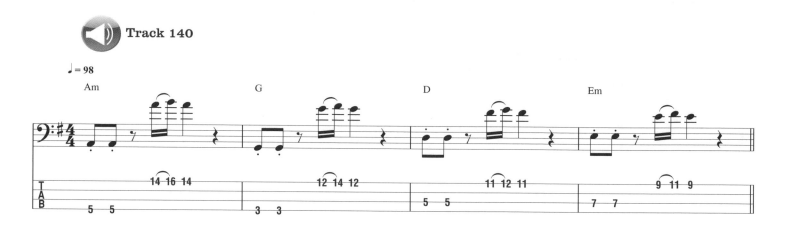

The Mixolydian Scale

The Mixolydian scale—the fifth mode of the major scale—is one of the most popular modal scales used by bass players. The modes are an extensive study all on their own and represent more material that we can cover in this book. However, the Mixolydian mode is commonly used to create melody in bass lines, and it's worth including in this chapter. The half step and whole step formula for Mixolydian is very similar to the major scale, with the exception of a flatted seventh. This makes the scale ideal to play against dominant seventh chords and, when played in major keys, mellows the sing-songy effect that the seventh step of the regular major scale creates. The Mixolydian scale is the go-to scale for many players, from Duff McKagen to Geddy Lee.

Here's one octave of the G Mixolydian scale, which is relative to the C major scale and therefore contains no sharps or flats.

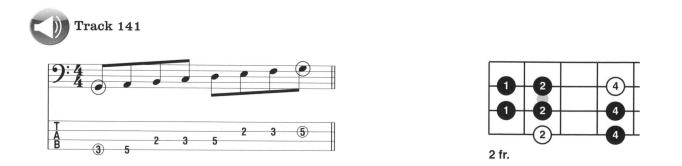

The following Mixolydian riff is reminiscent of Aerosmith's "Sweet Emotion" and utilizes many of the notes of the scale to create a melodic bass figure.

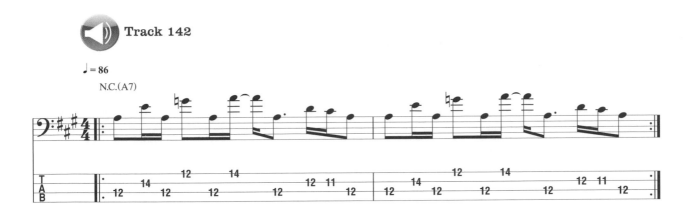

Here's a I–IV progression in D major that uses the D Mixolydian scale for its melodies instead of the regular major scale. John Paul Jones or Geddy Lee might use this approach when employing the Mixolydian mode in a major key.

The major and minor scales (as well as the modes) can be used effectively to add melody to bass lines, but it's important to know the basic theory behind these scales in order to properly apply them. Once you've developed an ear for the scales, you can use your instincts to bend these theoretical rules. The most successful melodic lines will weave themselves through a chord progression without straying too far from the harmonic structure or obscuring the groove. Paul McCartney is a master of melody on the bass, and his gift for playing melodic bass lines has influenced virtually every one of his contemporaries. Studying the bass lines from The Beatles catalog is a great place to start.

CHROMATIC PASSING TONES

The use of chromatic notes is very common in bass lines of all styles. Chromatic *passing tones* can be used to connect from chord to chord in a progression the notes within arpeggios and scales. In this chapter, we'll explore some of the most popular uses of chromatic passing tones.

Passing Tones in Progressions

A simple way to use a passing tone effectively is to place it between the chords of a progression when moving from one root note to the next. This is demonstrated in the second measure of the following example by inserting the note D♭ just before switching from the Dm chord to the C chord. Another type of chromatic device, called a *neighbor tone*, is also used here in the fifth and sixth measures on the B♭ chord, where the bass descends a half step to the note A and then moves back up to B♭.

Track 144

This next example demonstrates how you can connect the root notes in a simple, power-chord progression. The first two measures demonstrate the line without the passing tones; the second two measures incorporate chromatic passing tones.

Track 145

Passing Tones in Arpeggios

Connecting the notes in an arpeggio with chromatic passing tones is also a popular move, especially in old-school rock and walking bass. This next example is a ♭VII–IV–I rock progression in the key of E major that's set up perfectly to use major arpeggios with chromatic passing tones on each chord.

Track 146

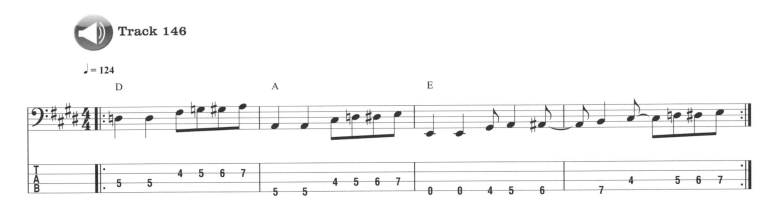

Here's another example using a I–V progression in D major. The bass line starts on the root note (D), drops down to the 3rd (F♯), and climbs chromatically up to the 5th (A), which is also the root note of the V chord.

Track 147

The Blues Scale

The most popular chromatic passing tone is the addition of the ♭5th to the minor pentatonic scale, which turns it into a blues scale. This additional note is commonly referred to as the *blues tri-tone*. Here's one octave of the A blues scale, starting at the fifth fret on the fourth string.

The A Blues Scale

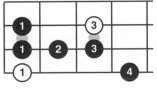

5 fr.

Here's an example of the blues scale being used in the key of A minor. This blues-rock riff features a descending blues scale and syncopation.

Track 148

Let's transpose the blues scale to the key of E minor and play it in open position. This example is played in a shuffle feel and features a descending quarter-note triplet fill in the last measure.

Track 149

Let's try another example in E minor that utilizes the notes of the blues scale in a different position, with the majority of the riff played up around the fifth fret.

Track 150

The blues tri-tone can also be used as a neighbor tone in bass riffs. The following riff gives us an opportunity to use some additional techniques. The basic riff is shown four different ways: plucking each note, using a hammer-on and pull-off combination, using a bend, and using a quick legato slide. Notice how each of these techniques can add a unique flavor to an otherwise simple blues riff.

In addition to the blues tri-tone, it's common to add a passing tone between the ♭7th and the octave of the scale. The following example demonstrates this in the key of A minor over a descending i–VII–VI–v chord progression. The riff at the end of each of the first three measures is repeated as a theme, followed by a traditional blues lick at the end of the fourth measure.

The Major Blues Scale

There's also a relative major version of the blues scale, based on the major pentatonic scale with a chromatic passing tone between the second and third steps of the scale. Here's one octave of the G major blues scale.

The G Major Blues Scale

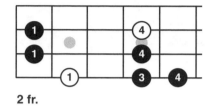

2 fr.

You'll notice that the above fingering is a bit uncomfortable, since the three-note chromatic passage gets split between the third and fourth strings. When using the scale for riffs and bass lines, it's more economical to shift positions as shown below. Start out with your first finger on the root note, G, at the third fret and then slide up two frets to play the rest of the scale.

The G Major Blues Scale

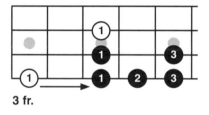

3 fr.

Here's an example of a bass riff using the above G major blues scale fingering.

🔊 **Track 153**

♩ = 116

N.C.(G)

We can also insert a second chromatic passing tone as we did with the minor blues scale. In the major version, the other passing tone occurs between the fifth and sixth steps of the scale. The following example is a slight variation of the above bass line that incorporates the additional chromatic passing tone.

Track 154

The major blues scale works very well in open position too; here's an example in the key of E major. You can also transpose and play this riff in A major by moving the entire pattern up one string.

Track 155

Some major blues riffs also incorporate the dominant seventh (♭7th). Adding this note produces a type of hybrid major/minor blues scale. Here's an example that's reminiscent of the riff from "Day Tripper" by The Beatles.

Track 156

Chromatic passing tones are effective and easy to use when constructing your bass lines or improvising. Since these notes fall outside of the regular scale and chord tones, you can play them just about anywhere without having to be concerned with all of the music theory. The most common chromatic passing tones are used in the blues scales, made popular by many rock and metal bands— from Aerosmith to Guns N' Roses.

STYLISTIC BASS LINES

Let's tie all of the elements from the previous chapters together and explore the bass styles of some of the great rock masters. The theoretical knowledge presented in this book can be used to dissect the bass lines of your favorite players and give you the tools you'll need to emulate them and construct your own unique bass parts.

John Paul Jones

Bassist John Paul Jones of Led Zeppelin was one of the bass greats of the '70s. Influenced by early Motown, blues, and soul, he was a master of groove and improvisation. By taking these elements and applying them in a hard rock and metal context, Jones and drummer John Bonham created one of the most dynamic rock rhythm sections of all time.

This first example is inspired by the chorus section of "Communication Breakdown." The song is in the key of E, with Jones doubling the heavy guitar riff during the verses using just the root notes, but once the chorus hits, he takes off running on the IV and V chords, playing arpeggios with chromatic passing tones, the blues scale, and the Mixolydian scale.

Track 157

John Paul Jones was also adept at coming up with great melodic bass hooks that breathe life into mellow verses. The next passage is similar to the verse in "Ramble On" and uses the notes of the major pentatonic scale against a simple I–IV chord progression.

Track 158

This next bass line uses the Mixolydian scale and some chromatic passing tones to establish a blues figure in the key of E major. In cases like this, Jones would usually set up a basic motif and use it as a starting point, gradually altering it throughout the song.

Track 159

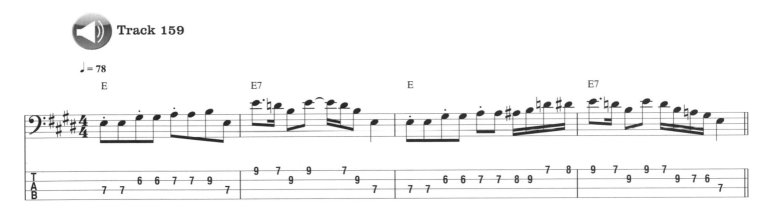

Geezer Butler

Black Sabbath's Geezer Butler is a heavy metal innovator, often considered to be the godfather of metal bass. His grungy bass tone complements the Sabbath sound and has influenced metal bassists for decades. On early Black Sabbath recordings, Butler was a master of the pentatonic and blues scales, incorporating distortion and wah-wah with heavy blues influences to create his unique style.

This first example, played in the style of "N.I.B.," uses the notes of the E minor pentatonic and a classic bend up to the ♭5th.

Track 160

This next example showcases Butler's heavy R&B influence. The bass line is played with a shuffle feel and is reminiscent of something he would improvise during an instrumental section in the key of G minor.

Track 161

Here's an example of a melodic bass line played around a root–5th–octave figure. The basic pattern is repeated over each chord of a i–VII–VI–V progression in the key of E minor.

Track 162

Flea

Bassist Flea from the Red Hot Chili Peppers is one of the more influential contemporary bass players to emerge in the 1990s. Flea earned a reputation for his slapping chops and funk influences, but he's also a master of melodic rock improvisation.

Here's an example in the style of "Dani California" that shows how Flea might play over a simple minor progression and add some tasty melodic runs using the minor pentatonic scale.

Track 163

Here's a funky bass line in G major that uses the notes of the Mixolydian scale. Flea plays the lower notes on the kick drums to establish the groove and alternately jumps up to the 12th fret to add in a few melodic riffs in between.

Track 164

Tom Hamilton

Tom Hamilton of Aerosmith is one of the great unsung bass heroes to come out of the fertile rock scene of the '70s. Many rock bass players have since pointed to Hamilton as a big influence due to his excellent instincts, rock-solid groove, pocket playing, and successful songwriting.

Here's an example of a funky bass line in the style of "Walk This Way." The bass combines elements of the major and minor blues scale and the Mixolydian scale, along with tasteful chromatic passing tones.

Track 165

This next example is played with a blues shuffle and uses the notes of an Em7 arpeggio. In the last measure, there's a nice triplet riff on a descending E blues scale.

Track 166

Duff McKagan

Duff McKagan, the original bassist of Guns N' Roses, has a pretty straight-ahead rock style and does a good job of locking in with the kick drum, while also managing to add some melody and pentatonic riffs to his bass lines.

This example is similar to the bass in "Sweet Child O' Mine." It features a pretty straightforward rock groove and a I–♭VII–IV progression with some tasteful melodic passages and chromatic passing tones.

Track 167

Duff can often be heard utilizing the blues scales. One signature move that comes up in his bass lines involves the use of a hammer-on from the minor 3rd to the major 3rd, regardless of whether the song is in a major or minor key. The following example is reminiscent of the bridge in "Mr. Brownstone," and this riff style can also be heard in the bass line from "Rocket Queen."

Track 168

Tony Kanal

No Doubt's bassist, Tony Kanal, incorporates elements of rock, punk, funk, and reggae to craft his prominent and challenging bass lines. He often cites Flea as a big influence, but it's clear that he digs much deeper into a variety of bass masters for his inspiration.

Here's an example in the style of the chorus to "Just a Girl," where Kanal plays the root notes of the i–VII–VI–VII progression on the kick drums for beats 1 and 3 and adds a repeated sixteenth-note motif on beats 2 and 4.

Track 169

This next example is reminiscent of the chorus from "Don't Speak." In this rock ballad, Kanal plays a Latin feel with elements of reggae, contributing a groove that really makes the chorus pop.

Track 170

Paul McCartney

From his work with The Beatles to his band Wings, Paul McCartney is probably the most influential bass player in rock history. His instinct for constructing perfect melodic bass lines has been studied by rock bassists from every generation and genre.

Here's an example that shows how McCartney would often come up with a pentatonic riff and transpose it for each chord of the progression. This idea can be heard in "Day Tripper," "Drive My Car," and "Taxman."

Track 171

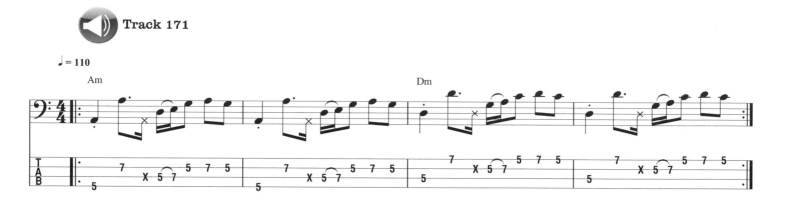

This next example is reminiscent of the verse from Lennon's "A Day in the Life." McCartney uses chord inversions here to play a smooth, descending bass melody. At the end of the second and fourth measures, there's some featured syncopation that occurs right where the vocal rests.

Track 172

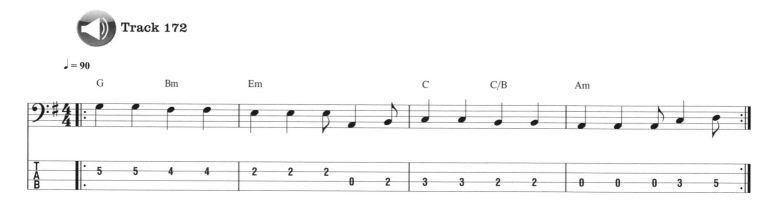

Here's a bass line that's similar to the verse of "You Won't See Me." Here, McCartney establishes a melody using simple arpeggios.

Track 173

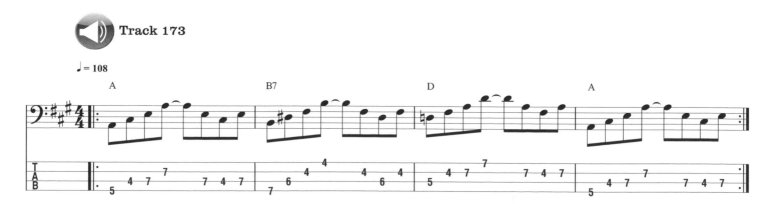

John Entwistle

The Who's bassist John Entwistle had a bright treble tone and an active fingerstyle technique that gave his playing one of the most unique and recognizable bass sounds. His busy, syncopated playing style clashed considerably with drummer Keith Moon's over-the-top theatrical style, yet somehow they came together to create a brilliant and creative rhythm section.

The following example is similar to one of Entwistle's greatest bass lines, featured in the song "The Real Me." The intro and middle sections have minor pentatonic and blues scale solos that span the entire range of the instrument.

Track 174

This next example showcases Entwistle's knack for manipulating the pentatonic scale into an effective melody. At first glance, this is simply the descending notes of an A major pentatonic scale, with the chord progression switching between D and A chords. If we take a closer look, though, you can see that Entwistle starts each measure on the note F♯, which is the 3rd of the D major chord. In the first and third measures, the bass lands on the root note, A, when the chord changes to A major on beat 3. However, in the second and fourth measures, he employs syncopation, and the bass ends up playing the note C♯—the 3rd of the A major chord—when the chord changes. Even though it isn't necessary to think through the process in this much detail, by analyzing the line we can see exactly why it works so well here.

Track 175

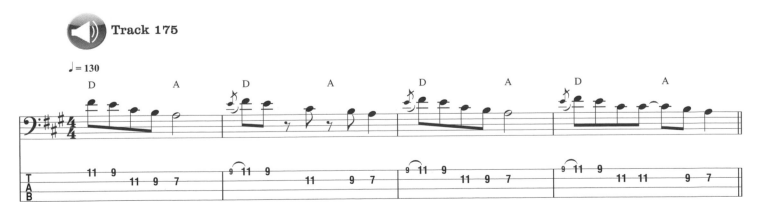

PLAY-ALONG TRACKS

The following play-along tracks feature many of the beats and chord progressions used for the examples in this book. Each track contains drums and rhythm guitar without any bass, giving you space to write, practice, or improvise your own bass lines. When working with these tracks, first determine the beat, key, and chord progression, and then try to apply the many different scales, arpeggios, and techniques covered in the previous chapters. Each example is repeated multiple times, giving you plenty of room to try out different ideas.

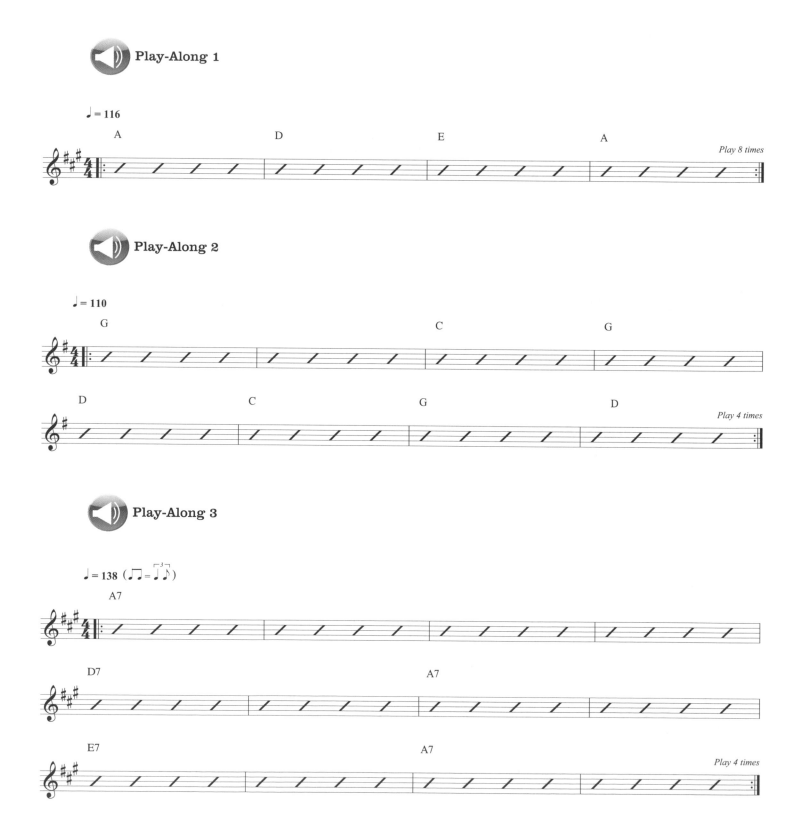

 **Play-Along 4**

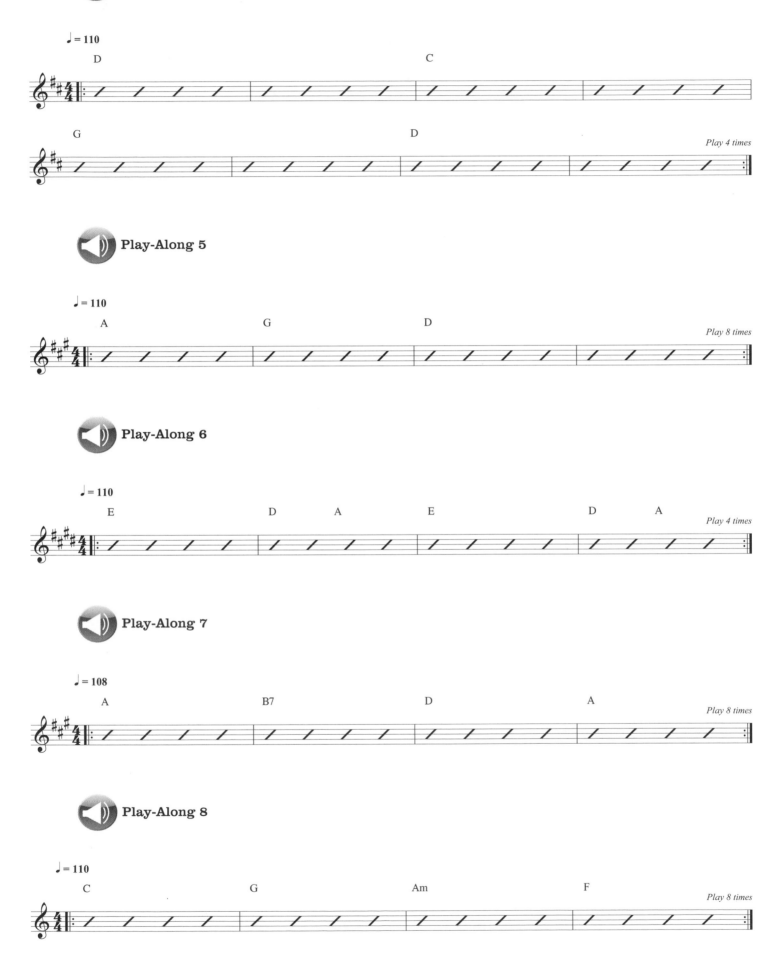

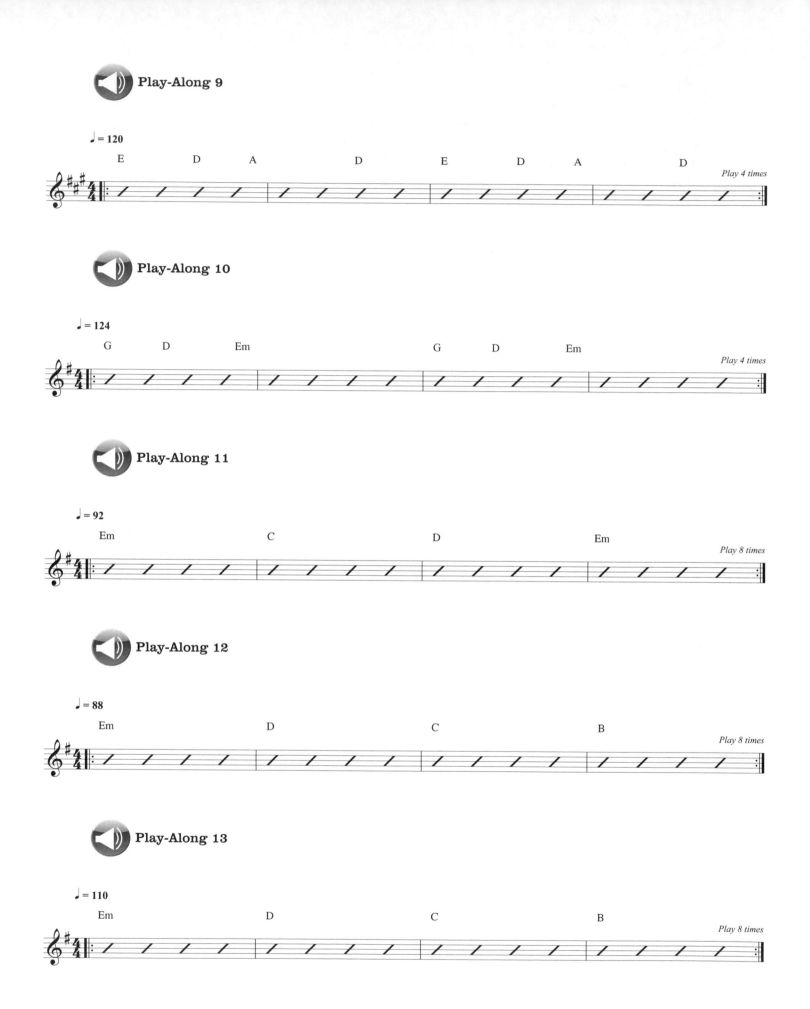

How To Create Rock Bass Lines

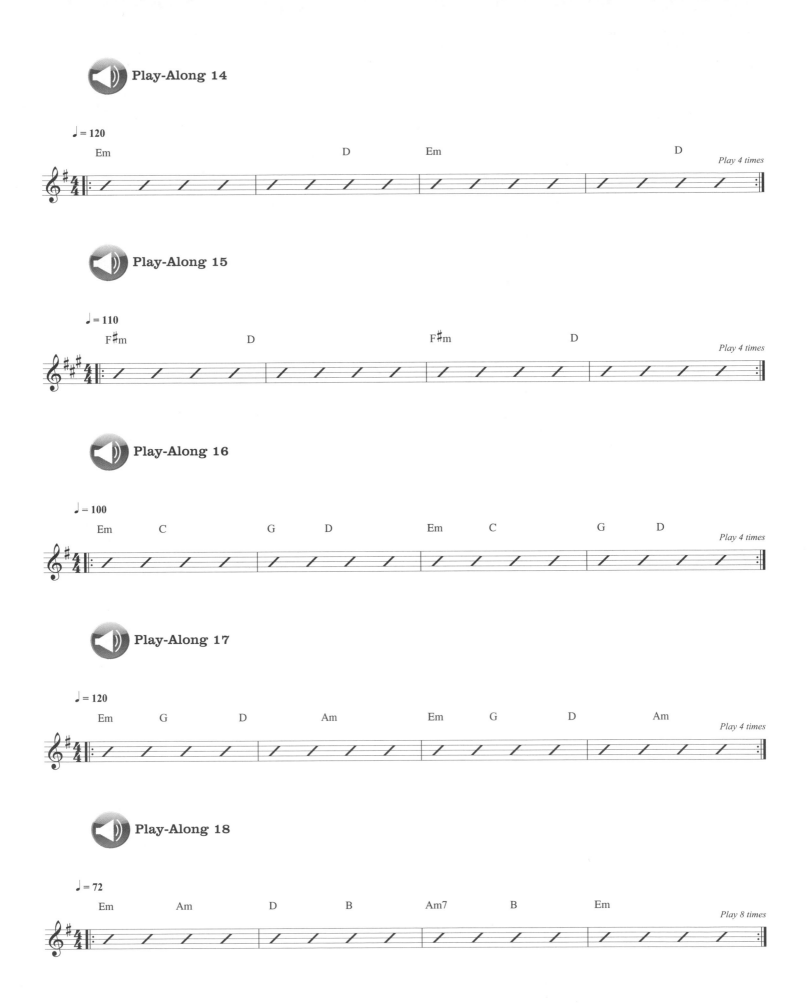

BASS RECORDED VERSIONS

Bass Recorded Versions feature authentic transcriptions written in standard notation and tablature for bass guitar. This series features complete bass lines from the classics to contemporary superstars.

**25 All-Time
Rock Bass Classics**
00690445 / $14.95

**25 Essential
Rock Bass Classics**
00690210 / $15.95

**Avenged Sevenfold –
Nightmare**
00691054 / $19.99

Bass Tab 1990-1999
00690400 / $16.95

Bass Tab 1999-2000
00690404 / $14.95

Bass Tab 2013
00121899 / $19.99

Bass Tab White Pages
00690508 / $29.99

The Beatles – Abbey Road
00128336 / $22.99

The Beatles Bass Lines
00690170 / $14.95

The Beatles 1962-1966
00690556 / $18.99

The Beatles 1967-1970
00690557 / $19.99

The Best of Blink 182
00690549 / $18.95

Best of Bass Tab
00141806 / $14.99

Blues Bass Classics
00690291 / $14.95

Boston Bass Collection
00690935 / $19.95

The Best of Eric Clapton
00660187 / $19.95

Stanley Clarke Collection
00672307 / $19.95

**Dream Theater
Bass Anthology**
00119345 / $24.99

Funk Bass Bible
00690744 / $19.95

Hard Rock Bass Bible
00690746 / $17.95

**Jimi Hendrix –
Are You Experienced?**
00690371 / $17.95

Incubus – Morning View
00690639 / $17.95

**Iron Maiden Bass
Anthology**
00690867 / $22.99

Jazz Bass Classics
00102070 / $17.99

Best of Kiss for Bass
00690080 / $19.95

**Lynyrd Skynyrd –
All-Time Greatest Hits**
00690956 / $19.99

Bob Marley Bass Collection
00690568 / $19.95

Mastodon – Crack the Skye
00691007 / $19.99

Megadeth Bass Anthology
00691191 / $19.99

Metal Bass Tabs
00103358 / $19.99

Best of Marcus Miller
00690811 / $24.99

Motown Bass Classics
00690253 / $14.95

Muse Bass Tab Collection
00123275 / $19.99

Nirvana Bass Collection
00690066 / $19.95

No Doubt – Tragic Kingdom
00120112 / $22.95

**The Offspring –
Greatest Hits**
00690809 / $17.95

**Jaco Pastorius –
Greatest Jazz Fusion
Bass Player**
00690421 / $19.99

The Essential Jaco Pastorius
00690420 / $19.99

Pearl Jam – Ten
00694882 / $16.99

**Pink Floyd –
Dark Side of the Moon**
00660172 / $14.95

The Best of Police
00660207 / $14.95

Pop/Rock Bass Bible
00690747 / $17.95

Queen – The Bass Collection
00690065 / $19.99

R&B Bass Bible
00690745 / $17.95

Rage Against the Machine
00690248 / $17.99

**The Best of
Red Hot Chili Peppers**
00695285 / $24.95

**Red Hot Chili Peppers –
Blood Sugar Sex Magik**
00690064 / $19.95

**Red Hot Chili Peppers –
By the Way**
00690585 / $19.95

**Red Hot Chili Peppers –
Californication**
00690390 / $19.95

**Red Hot Chili Peppers –
Greatest Hits**
00690675 / $18.95

**Red Hot Chili Peppers –
I'm with You**
00691167 / $22.99

**Red Hot Chili Peppers –
One Hot Minute**
00690091 / $18.95

**Red Hot Chili Peppers –
Stadium Arcadium**
00690853 / $24.95

**Red Hot Chili Peppers –
Stadium Arcadium:
Deluxe Edition**
Book/2-CD Pack
00690863 / $39.95

Rock Bass Bible
00690446 / $19.95

Rolling Stones
00690256 / $16.95

**Sly & The Family Stone
for Bass**
00109733 / $19.99

**Stevie Ray Vaughan –
Lightnin' Blues 1983-1987**
00694778 / $19.95

Best of Yes
00103044 / $19.99

Best of ZZ Top for Bass
00691069 / $22.99

HAL•LEONARD®
CORPORATION
7777 W. BLUEMOUND RD. P.O. BOX 13819 MILWAUKEE, WI 53213

Visit Hal Leonard Online at
www.halleonard.com

Prices, contents & availability subject to change without notice.
Some products may not be available outside the U.S.A.

1015